Searching for
Mary Magdalene:

HER STORY OF AWARENESS, ACCEPTANCE AND ACTION

Lynne —

Enjoy Reading!

Soni Werner

Published by Fountain Publishing®
P.O. Box 80011, Rochester, Michigan 48308-0011
www.fountainpublishing.com

Manufactured in the United States of America by Fountain Publishing

Cover photo artwork by Soni S. Werner
Book design by Karin A. Childs

Soni S. Werner,
Searching For Mary Magdalene/ Soni S. Werner

ISBN 10: 1-936665-03-4
ISBN 13: 978-1936665-03-7

SEARCHING FOR
MARY MAGDALENE:

Her Story of Awareness, Acceptance, and Action

BY SONI S. WERNER, PhD

Fountain Publishing®
Rochester, Michigan

With Gratitude

I would like to thank the following people and organizations that helped me in this project.

* The staff of the Glencairn Museum who organized the guided trip to France to see medieval cathedrals. The Director of the Glencairn Museum, Stephen Morley, also permitted me to investigate artifacts in the Museum illustrating Mary Magdalene. I have included two photographs of stained glass windows, crafted by Winfred Hyatt.

* Rev. Eric Carswell and the Carpenter Fund which gave me financial support during my travels to France and Israel.

* The Lemole family who gave me financial support during my travels to England.

* My international travel guides: Lisa, Richard, Michael and Shmuel.

* My art teachers: Wendy Soneson, Frank Rose, Tom Rose and Lisa Knight.

* The hundreds of artists and craftspeople who made images of Mary Magdalene for our benefit. When I knew their names I gave them credit in this book.

* The unknown, modern-day sculptor who made a copper casting of a Woman from the Bible, and displayed it in a public street of Jerusalem. I have painted my version of this lovely piece of art, and assumed it could be an image of Mary Magdalene. It appears on the cover of this book and at the beginning of each chapter.

* The faculty and deans of Bryn Athyn College, who gave me a sabbatical during spring term 2011 to write my book.

* Rev. Jeremy Simons who helped me understand the spiritual meaning of a person feeling "possessed by demons"

* My husband, Neil, who always encouraged me in my relentless pursuit of Mary Magdalene.

CONTENTS:

INTRODUCTION

I yearn for a role model. This may sound odd coming from a woman nearing retirement age, but I see myself as no different from most women who learn how to live well by observing amazing females. I needed different types of role models when I was a teenager. I looked to movie stars and older female cousins to get an idea of how to really flourish. They led me to learn how to surf in California (thanks to "Gidget," played by Sally Field), and then they encouraged me to imagine that I could actually go to college, after my surfing days were done (thanks to cousins Tryn and Dorothy). In my early adulthood, I searched for role models on how to be a good wife, a mother, and a college professor. Most people need role models, but we tend to seek out different ones at the various stages of our lives. These selected role models have faced challenges like the ones we are currently tackling, but we like the way they manage these obstacles with such finesse and grace. They inspire us with their courage and tenacity. These role models could be currently living down the street from us, or known from afar through the media, or studied in history books. They could be our imaginary friends.

This book is about my yearning for a spiritual role model, especially during the decade of my 50's. I invite you into the story of my search. Pretend you are looking over my shoulder as I searched. Perhaps you will come to deeply appreciate the role model I selected, or just learn a procedure for how to really study the one you select to enrich your life. I feel pretty confident that if you identify a specific role model, learn about her, and then imagine how you could be more like her, that it will help you find your way whenever you feel lost.

My story picks up after I had narrowed the field down to one individual. I won't bore you with the details of my long consideration of many current and historical female figures. That part of the search was important to me, and I encourage you, the reader, to make your own selection of an intriguing role model who might guide you on your life's journey. But I think my story got much more interesting once I decided to focus on really investigating and reflecting on the life of Mary Magdalene. Welcome to my story of learning about her. It is ongoing, but this is a progress report.

Of course, I am not the first person to select Mary Magdalene to serve in this role in my life. She lived 2000 years ago, and millions of men and women have studied her, painted images of her, prayed to her, and made up stories about her to fill their needs. Perhaps each of us have felt: "I think I really GET her . . . I understand what she was experiencing, and I can draw strength from empathizing with her during her struggles and joys." So I'm not the first. Oh well. Doesn't matter. In fact it makes my search to understand her much more interesting!

One advantage of choosing a well-known role model is that there are plenty of resource materials to read about her. But the disadvantage is also that there are plenty of resource materials to read . . . and they disagree with each other! I have discovered that I can't rely on just one source, such as a scholarly-type book, a Gospel of the *Holy Bible*, an ancient document written on papyrus, a website, a cathedral window, or a brochure about her relics, and then claim that I now know all there is to know about her. I need plenty of sources and then I need to sort through them all. So I have been traveling around France, England, Israel and America to see sacred art and architecture related to Mary Magdalene. I have been gathering books, studying, comparing, reflecting, and then going to painting classes to learn how to express what I think she felt through my portraits of her. Now I am writing and speaking about her life and what she means to me. Never have I had such a comprehensive experience on one topic, involving so many aspects of my life:

* My professional work as a psychologist.
* My love of traveling to remarkable places.
* My evolution as an adult female.
* My creative hobby as a painter.
* My venture into becoming a writer.
* My own spiritual regeneration.

Usually these parts of my life are rather disconnected. It has added to my joy and intensity: to learn about her, critically compare the different legends and doctrines, and then express in prayers, words and images what she means to me.

I am also partly motivated to study her in order to pull myself away from focusing on other role models promoted by the current media: movie stars, authors of novels, and scholars in my field. They each have their lovely qualities that I appreciate, and I am inspired by them. But there is a limit, and I soon tire of them. I need a role model with some depth!

I remember when I first realized that there weren't very many leading female characters in the Bible or fairy tales. My study of Mary Magdalene is also part of a life-long search for brave girls and women in stories. Too often females were left out of the stories that were read to me, or the girl characters were passive, fearful people who needed protection. I loved it when I saw new children's books being written with more female lead characters than I ever read when I was growing up (before the Women's Movement of the 1960's). I read these new fables and realistic fiction to my two daughters, who have now grown up to become confident, brave women working in New York City. Stories have power.

I also got excited when the book *The Red Tent* came out, because it elaborated on the Biblical story of the sons of Israel, from a sister's point of view![1] I know it was historical fiction, but it stirred my curiosity and helped me explore other females in the Bible. Stories matter, especially to women. The female role models in these stories help us when our imaginations and courage are in short supply.

So, who was Mary Magdalene, and how am I learning about her? I am approaching this investigation of her by using my favorite tools. I was trained to be a college professor of psychology, and in my college classes I use several tools that I am also employing as I study her. Allow me to tell you about those tools, briefly for now, and know that I will bring them up repeatedly throughout the book in much more detail. If you ever need more background on these tools, you can investigate the references and endnotes. I will also break up the flow of the narrative occasionally and highlight a specific tool: it might be a focus on a psychological theory or a spiritual concept that I have learned. You can use these same tools in your own analysis of a role model. Feel free to skip around in the book and just focus on these highlighted sections, if all you want are the tools. Here they are, gathered and organized for your enjoyment. I do not take credit for the creation of these tools, but I share my enthusiasm with you about how I am using them to more deeply appreciate Mary Magdalene. I invite you to see what excitement I have in the application of these much loved tools in my search and study of a wonderful role model.

These tools come from psychology, philosophy and theology. I will explain these concepts, first in their creators' terminology and then I will re-state them in more plain English. Sometimes I use a theory like a lens: a tool that enables me to examine her life more carefully. Other times, I use a concept as a way of explaining my own procedure for sorting through all the conflicting material about Mary Magdalene. These theories and concepts help me make sense of what is going on. I gain empathy or a logical perspective, and both are helpful.

I have taught most of these ideas to my students, but if you are not currently taking a psychology class you may not be aware of them. They are wonderful tools, but they could be refined, and maybe you will be the one to redesign one of them as you try them out, and see their strengths and weaknesses. I have also attempted to create a theory of my own based on a unique synthesis of psychology, philosophy and theology, which I include near the end of this book. It is a new tool, not yet worn from use, so it needs some refinement. I encourage you to examine, critique, refine or create your own theories to help you make sense of the world around you.

To give you an example, Harry Moody is a modern-day philosopher who has studied men and women in the last decades of their lives. After listening to many elders, he created a theory called the *Stages of the Soul*.[2] So here is a philosophical tool that helps us name the five predictable stages that people usually experience while they are on their spiritual journeys. If we learn Moody's five stages, it is like learning the itinerary of a previous traveler, and we can experience the trip vicariously and mindfully. I will apply Moody's theory to my understanding of Mary Magdalene's life and my own. As with all good tools, this one by Moody can be transferred to new situations and used over and over. Each time I apply it, I gain more appreciation for the depth of this philosophical tool.

So I will describe, explain and apply many theories and concepts to my understanding and appreciation of Mary Magdalene. Through this process I will testify to the influence she is having on me, in my psychological, philosophical and spiritual life. I will review some well-known ideas about her life, critique the legends that I find less credible, and offer a fresh new spiritual perspective, as well.

 I have placed images and icons throughout the book. Whenever I am drawing a theory or concept from the field of psychology, I'll include an image of the Greek letter "PSI" to remind you of psychology.

 Then whenever I draw ideas from philosophy, I'll include the Greek letter "PHI."

Finally, whenever I draw concepts from theology, I'll include the Greek letter: "THETA."

Hopefully, this will make it easy for you to quickly locate these concepts and theories. In addition, I have decided to use visual images as icons at the beginning of sections when I am telling my personal journey or when I am giving information about Mary Magdalene. I have felt very much like a pilgrim wandering to sacred places across the globe so I have decided to borrow the image of a shell and placed it before sections of narration about my pilgrimages.

 The shell, notably the cockleshell or the scallop shell, is generally used in Catholic art to signify pilgrimage. The scallop shell is used specifically as an attribute of St. James the Great. It is generally supposed to allude to the countless pilgrimages made to his celebrated shrine at Compostella in Spain. St. Roch is customarily painted in the dress of a pilgrim with cockleshells in his hat. And the scallop shell is associated with St. John the Baptist because he baptized Christ. Most paintings depicting this scene in the life of Christ have the Baptist holding a shell from which water is pouring forth.[3]

So, although I am not interested in walking to see the Spanish site at Santiago de Compostella commemorating this martyr (St. James), I am borrowing the metaphorical image of the shell to depict my own personal travels to find Mary Magdalene. I did not actually carry a scallop shell with me, but I did wear a necklace with a tiny scallop shaped charm on it to keep me safe during my journey! Look for this image of the scallop shell in this book to find sections where I am telling about my own journey.

 I also wanted to have an image that would alert you that I am sharing information about Mary Magdalene, so in those sections of the book I will start with my painting of a stone sculpture found in the region of her home village of Magdala. Historians believe this image was part of a pediment over a doorway to a place of worship built around the time that Jesus and Mary Magdalene were living in Israel. It is possible that Jesus and Mary Magdalene actually saw this floral image in stone every time they went to the local temples near the Sea of Galilee during Jesus' ministry.[4]

I hope that as you read that you will vicariously enjoy my process of:

* Sorting through the stories that people have
   attributed to her
* Peeling away the less believable tales
* Confirming the most important elements of the
   stories
* Discovering some new theological interpretations
* Analyzing her objectively
* Empathizing with her subjectively
* Drawing courage from her character

MARY MAGDALENE AT THE CROSS, FRANCE

CHAPTER 1

How Do We Know About Mary Magdalene?

I first became aware of Mary Magdalene when I attended Church and Sunday School lessons as a child. She seemed to be a minor character in the Easter story. We recited passages from the Gospels of the New Testament and sang songs that still stir my heart in church each Easter. I think one of my favorites went: "When very early in the dawn, weeping they came and found Him gone . . . Lo an angel, stood before them. 'Seek Him not among the dead. For He is risen as He said, Allelujah, Allelujah.' "[5] I loved getting dressed up for Easter in my special pastel dress and carrying flowers to contribute to the church. The altar girls would collect them and I knew church volunteers would donate these flowers to sick people in the hospitals that afternoon. Our family would hide Easter baskets and candy. We dyed eggs and ate way too many chocolate bunnies. Relatives and friends would gather and have a lovely meal.

So I have pretty happy memories of learning as a child about Mary Magdalene in the context of the joy of Easter morning. Our emphasis was more on the risen Lord than on His suffering on the cross. In fact, I don't remember ever seeing an image of Jesus dying on the cross in the Christian churches of my childhood. I do remember a day when I was about seven years old and I was sitting at the dining room table with paper and crayons, drawing pictures of Easter. Of course, I drew the Easter Bunny and his big basket of candy,

WERNER AS A CHILD ON EASTER, 1956 MICHIGAN USA

but then I drew both the crucifixion scene and the sepulcher scene. I distinctly recall my mother telling me that she did not want me to draw the sad scene of the crucifixion, but she liked my illustration of Easter morning. So I was being taught at an early age which part of the religious Easter story to emphasize. One image was taboo and the other appreciated. I did not understand at the time, but I did what I was told. I threw out the picture of Jesus on the cross and did not attempt to draw that scene again for over fifty years.

When I look back on these experiences of my childhood, I can see that I was dealing with several things: the various parts of the religious Easter story with the events involving Jesus and Mary Magdalene, and the non-religious, playful parts of the Easter holiday (bunnies, eggs, flowers, dresses). I was much more interested in the playful parts of Easter when I was a child, but it left an impression on me that Easter was worth celebrating and I had a tiny clue about its importance. Having special foods, songs, clothes and ceremonies became my foundation for learning about my faith in a very tangible way. I experienced something concrete which was associated with something abstract that I did not yet understand. Perhaps you have your own childhood memories of Easter that are a combination of your feelings, thoughts, tastes, sounds, sights, and recollections of social gatherings and religious activities.

PSYCHOLOGICAL TOOL
In the 1980's, Dr. James Fowler, a developmental psychologist, described six stages of the development of faith. He said that children age two to seven are in the first stage called "Intuitive-Projective Faith". Young children are full of fantasy, stories, images and ideas taught to them, by their parents and early elementary teachers. He terms it Intuitive because their minds are full of images and symbols from complex stories that fascinate them intuitively, but that they probably would not be able to retell to others. The children know these symbols are important based on what has been taught to them but they are

not sure why the visual symbols hold such importance. He calls it Projective Faith because young children project their egocentric ideas onto other people and assume everyone sees the world as they see it. They cannot conceive of the idea that other people might see the world differently than they do. In the second stage according to Fowler, children aged seven to ten are in "Mythic-Literal Faith". At this point, children can comprehend an entire story from beginning to end, and become aware that it has meaning for their own lives. They still love symbols and dramatic events in their myths and stories, but they cannot yet reflect on any deep correspondence of the symbols. They love heroes and sympathize with the characters in the stories. As they learn the stories of their faith tradition, they emphasize the literal sense of the good winning out over the bad characters in their powerful conflicts. They do not understand how one character could have both good and bad in her personality.[6]

 My early Easter experiences would be typical of the stages of Intuitive-Projective or Mythic-Literal Faith, according to Fowler. I was hearing tales about people I could not see in person, but I was learning to memorize these intriguing stories and then recreate them in my artwork, dramatic plays and songs. My parents and Sunday School teachers clearly valued the Easter story and so I received faith from them. I was too young to question anything, and I followed along in their footsteps. I was a bit puzzled by the two stories—Easter Bunny and Jesus' resurrection—but no one else seemed upset by the juxtaposition. Soon I realized that I was hearing one story in church and the other NOT in church. That was about as much of a distinction as I could make. I handled the two Christmas stories of Santa and Jesus' birth in a like manner. We celebrated both on the same day, but with no logical connection between them.

This stage of childhood is precious and wonderful but it is developmentally appropriate only for very young people, not adults. However, in some faith traditions children and adults appear to be encouraged to stay stuck in these early stages. I notice that when I visit a Roman Catholic Mass that the clergy are addressed as Father and the leading nun is addressed as Mother. The clergy call the members of the congregation Children as they instruct them to memorize prayers, visit the Stations of the Cross, recite creeds and follow along in the Mass rituals. In fact, it was not until Vatican II in the 1960's that clergy permitted members to directly read the *Holy Bible* in English for themselves rather than just depending on the clergy to preach.[7]

I have visited many Catholic ceremonies as a non-member and have witnessed people of all ages being addressed by the clergy as if they were children in the Mythic-Literal Faith stage. Although I have no way of knowing the sincerity of each person's faith, I do think that there is very little encouragement for the laity to evolve to higher levels of reasoning in their faith. This paternalistic treatment might have been appropriate in the Middle Ages in Europe when most laity could not read, but now the vast majority are literate and can read and reflect on their personal faith. I encourage individuals of any church to move beyond the expectations of clergy who continue to treat laypeople like children. I believe this is especially important for women.

When it comes to analyzing important Biblical stories such as the resurrection of Jesus, it may feel blissful to just stay in the child-like stage by simply hearing the Gospel read in church. However, the more we make a mature effort to investigate the details and interpret the meaning for our lives, the richer our comprehension will be.

THEOLOGICAL TOOL
In the 1700's, Emanuel Swedenborg, a theologian and author, claims to have been guided by God to reveal and write down inner meaning of the literal Bible stories. The purpose of these Writings by Swedenborg is to explain Biblical stories at a very mature level and to teach us to reflect on how they can help us to live more meaningful lives. His work challenges us to move beyond a

child-like literalism with the Easter story. Swedenborg f
es on four specific events involving Mary Magdalene on
Easter morning. I will describe and explain these four events
with their internal sense from the Swedenborgian perspective,
in later chapters.[8]

 Before we go into the internal sense of the literal stories, let's review what the canonical Gospels of the Bible actually say about Mary Magdalene. The sacred texts of Matthew, Mark, Luke and John describe what she experienced. They vary in terms of the details that they include. Some of you may be more comfortable with a certain version of the *Holy Bible* and I realize that the following quotes may not be the same exact translation with which you are familiar. Some people call it the *Word,* and others call it the *Holy Bible.* I am quoting from the New International Version of the *Holy Bible* (2011) because I appreciate how it uses modern language but stays true to the story:

Matthew 28: 1-10
Mark 16: 1-11
Luke 24: 1-11
John 20: 1-18

After the Sabbath, at dawn on the first day of the week, Mary Magdalene and the other Mary went to look at the tomb. There was a violent earthquake, for an angel of the Lord came down from heaven and, going to the tomb, rolled back the stone and sat on it. His appearance was like lightning, and his clothes were white as snow. The guards were so afraid of him that they shook and became like dead men. The angel said to the women, "Do not be afraid, for I know that you are looking for Jesus, who was crucified. He is not here; he has risen, just as he said. Come and see the place where he lay. Then go quickly and tell his disciples: 'He has risen from the dead and is going ahead of you into Galilee. There you will see him.' Now I

have told you." So the women hurried away from the tomb, afraid yet filled with joy, and ran to tell his disciples. Suddenly Jesus met them. "Greetings," he said. They came to him, clasped his feet and worshiped him. Then Jesus said to them, "Do not be afraid. Go and tell my brothers to go to Galilee; there they will see me."
(Holy Bible: Matthew 28: 1-10)

When the Sabbath was over, Mary Magdalene, Mary the mother of James, and Salome bought spices so that they might go to anoint Jesus' body. Very early on the first day of the week, just after sunrise, they were on their way to the tomb and they asked each other, "Who will roll the stone away from the entrance of the tomb?" But when they looked up, they saw that the stone, which was very large, had been rolled away. As they entered the tomb, they saw a young man dressed in a white robe sitting on the right side, and they were alarmed. "Don't be alarmed," he said. "You are looking for Jesus the Nazarene, who was crucified. He has risen! He is not here. See the place where they laid him. But go, tell his disciples and Peter, 'He is going ahead of you into Galilee. There you will see him, just as he told you.'"Trembling and bewildered, the women went out and fled from the tomb. They said nothing to anyone, because they were afraid. When Jesus rose early on the first day of the week, he appeared first to Mary Magdalene, out of whom he had driven seven demons. She went and told those who had been with him and who were mourning and weeping. When they heard that Jesus was alive and that she had seen him, they did not believe it.
(Holy Bible, Mark 16: 1-11)

On the first day of the week, very early in the morning, the women took the spices they had prepared and went to the tomb. They found the stone rolled away from the tomb, but when they entered, they did not find the body of the Lord Jesus. While they were wondering about this,

suddenly two men in clothes that gleamed like lightning stood beside them. In their fright the women bowed down with their faces to the ground, but the men said to them, "Why do you look for the living among the dead? He is not here; he has risen! Remember how he told you, while he was still with you in Galilee: 'The Son of Man must be delivered over to the hands of sinners, be crucified and on the third day be raised again.' " Then they remembered his words. When they came back from the tomb, they told all these things to the Eleven and to all the others. It was Mary Magdalene, Joanna, Mary the mother of James, and the others with them who told this to the apostles. But they did not believe the women, because their words seemed to them like nonsense.
(Holy Bible: Luke 24:1-11)

Early on the first day of the week, while it was still dark, Mary Magdalene went to the tomb and saw that the stone had been removed from the entrance. So she came running to Simon Peter and the other disciple, the one Jesus loved, and said, "They have taken the Lord out of the tomb, and we don't know where they have put him!" So Peter and the other disciple started for the tomb. Both were running, but the other disciple outran Peter and reached the tomb first. He bent over and looked in at the strips of linen lying there but did not go in. Then Simon Peter came along behind him and went straight into the tomb. He saw the strips of linen lying there, as well as the cloth that had been wrapped around Jesus' head. The cloth was still lying in its place, separate from the linen. Finally the other disciple, who had reached the tomb first, also went inside. He saw and believed. (They still did not understand from Scripture that Jesus had to rise from the dead.) Then the disciples went back to where they were staying. Now Mary stood outside the tomb crying. As she wept, she bent over to look into the tomb and saw two angels in white, seated where Jesus' body had been, one at the head and the other at the foot. They asked her,

"Woman, why are you crying?" "They have taken my Lord away," she said, "and I don't know where they have put him." At this, she turned around and saw Jesus standing there, but she did not realize that it was Jesus. He asked her, "Woman, why are you crying? Who is it you are looking for?" Thinking he was the gardener, she said, "Sir, if you have carried him away, tell me where you have put him, and I will get him." Jesus said to her, "Mary." She turned toward him and cried out in Aramaic, "Rabboni!" (which means "Teacher"). Jesus said, "Do not hold on to me, for I have not yet ascended to the Father. Go instead to my brothers and tell them, 'I am ascending to my Father and your Father, to my God and your God.'" Mary Magdalene went to the disciples with the news: "I have seen the Lord!" And she told them that he had said these things to her.

(Holy Bible, John 24: 1-18)[9]

MARY MAGDALENE AT THE CROSS; PAINTING BY NICOT
TROYES, FRANCE

Women come to anoint the body of Jesus
Troyes, France

MARY MAGDALENE GREETS AN ANGEL, PAINTING BY NICOT
TROYES, FRANCE

JESUS APPEARS TO MARY MAGDALENE, PAINTING BY NICOT
TROYES, FRANCE

 When I read these four versions of the Easter story in the Holy Bible, I am intrigued by the similarities and differences. Notice that only one Gospel story refers to an earthquake. Some of the stories indicate that there were two angels appearing to Mary Magdalene and some say there was only one angel, but they are always dressed in gleaming white robes, as bright as lightening. In two of the Gospels there is a description of Jesus actually talking to Mary. In one case He is talking about His ascension and how she should not try to touch Him. But in the other He allows her to grasp His feet. In three of the Gospel stories, Jesus directs her to go tell the brethren about Him rising from the dead, but in one Gospel she says nothing because she is afraid.

These events happened nearly 2000 years ago. To make matters worse, scholars tell us that these stories were not actually written down immediately. One Gospel may have been written down around 70 - 100 AD, and another one about 30 years later. The others followed still later. Once all the various versions were put in writing, it was not until the fourth and fifth century AD that the New Testament of the *Holy Bible* became similar to the form that we know today. The Council of Nicea was gathered to make the plans for what documents would be included in the *Holy Bible* and which were considered too full of heresies to be included. It was a sorting process, and they had the influence of the newly organized Catholic Church and the authority of the emperor Constantine to enforce their decisions. If you disagreed you were in serious trouble and called a heretic. Christians were told to believe the canon: the accepted Gospels.[10]

Luckily, we live in the modern western world now and have more freedom of religion than people experienced in the first centuries after Jesus rose from the tomb. Our lives are not threatened if we have doubts or questions about the Easter story. We are free to read what we like and explore many resource materials that tell us about Jesus and Mary Magdalene. In addition to the four canonical Gospels, there are many other ways for us to learn about Mary Magdalene:

* Gnostic Gospels: hidden and recently found ancient documents

* Legends told during the Middle Ages in Europe

* Catholic Popes' sermons and declarations about Mary Magdalene's identity

* Paintings, statues, and stained glass images of her in cathedrals

* Historical fiction novels that combine the Bible story with invented literary fantasies

* Modern day scholars' books explaining the *Holy Bible*, ancient documents and legends

* Modern Broadway musicals and plays

* Modern documentaries and films, illustrating the stories

* New Age interpretations of history and theology

* Swedenborg's theological explanation of the internal meaning of the Bible stories which can help us grow spiritually

Just like the people in the Council of Nicea in 325 AD, we are permitted to decide what is credible and what is a heresy or even blasphemy. So how do we know what we know, and how do we justify what we decide to believe?

PHILOSOPHICAL TOOL
"Defined narrowly, epistemology is the study of knowledge and justified belief. As the study of knowledge, epistemology is concerned with the following questions: What are the necessary and

sufficient conditions of knowledge? What are its sources? What is its structure, and what are its limits? As the study of justified belief, epistemology aims to answer questions such as: How are we to understand the concept of justification? What makes justified beliefs justified? Is justification internal or external to one's own mind? Understood more broadly, epistemology is about issues having to do with the creation and dissemination of knowledge in particular areas of inquiry."[11]

 My particular area of inquiry is "who is Mary Magdalene and how do I justify what I think is credible information about her?" You can do the same as you study what you know about her, and you may or may not come to the same conclusions. This becomes an epistemological journey: how do I know what I know? As I mature beyond the mythic or child-like stage of just believing the stories and legends about her because people told them to me, I must deal with the unsettling feeling of not being sure of everything I read. This discomfort can make me want to regress back to the simpler time of just hearing Mary Magdalene's story on Easter Sunday and leaving it at that.

But the more I pay attention, the more I come to realize that not all these sources agree with each other! I am faced with not only noticing the differences between details in the stories in the four Gospels of the *Holy Bible*, but now I need to consider that there are other ancient documents worthy of my attention. There are ancient legends which people have embraced and believed for hundreds of years. Then in my lifetime, I have witnessed popular culture including Broadway plays (*Jesus Christ Superstar* and *Godspell*) and best-selling novels (*The DaVinci Code* and *The Book of Love*)[12] These well-known legends, plays and novels seem to be creative mixtures of doctrines and inventive elaborations. I am entertained and fascinated, but now I have dissonance in my mind. These versions are NOT in harmony with each other . . . so which version of Mary Magdalene is right?

Let's take one example: the Broadway musical play called *Jesus Christ Superstar*. This was written and first performed when I was in my adolescence and early adulthood in the 1970's. One of the very popular songs from this play was supposed to be Mary Magdalene singing about her relationship with Jesus Christ. Here are the lyrics:

"I don't know how to love him
What to do, how to move him
I've been changed, yes really changed
In these past few days
When I've seen myself
I seem like someone else
I don't know how to take this
I don't see why he moves me
He's a man
He's just a man
And I've had so many men before
In very many ways
He's just one more
Should I bring him down
Should I scream and shout
Should I speak of love
Let my feelings out?
I never thought I'd come to this
What's it all about?
Don't you think it's rather funny
I should be in this position?
I'm the one
Who's always been
So calm so cool
No lover's fool
Running every show
He scares me so
I never thought I'd come to this
What's it all about?
Yet if he said he loved me
I'd be lost

I'd be frightened
I couldn't cope
Just couldn't cope
I'd turn my head
I'd back away
I wouldn't want to know
He scares me so
I want him so
I love him so."[13]

Picture this: I am in my twenties living away from home at college and I hear this song from *Jesus Christ Superstar*. I am stunned. I get this intense impression that Mary Magdalene has a voice, and that she is telling us her confusion about her devotion to Jesus. Wait just a minute . . . Mary Magdalene is hardly ever actually quoted in the canonical Gospels. How do we know what she would have been saying? Is her devotion the same as falling in love with an ordinary man? Is she intrigued with how powerful and good He is, and what kind of magnetism He must have had for her? I go back to the *Holy Bible* and look for clues that she not only followed Him during his ministry, his death and burial, but that she might also be in love with Him. I could not find any indication of this kind of love. I start wondering about the different kinds of love and how she seems to be confusing them.

Φ PHILOSOPHICAL TOOL
The ancient and modern Greeks say that there are several different kinds of love: eros, philia, agape, storge and thelema. Eros is sensual or sexual desire. Philia means a virtuous kind of friendship love. Agape originates from God's love of all people and we can experience it as contentment when we look for the good in others. Storge means parental love. Finally, thelema is the passionate desire to be very involved in an activity.[14]

 How do I reconcile this song with what my Christian faith has taught me? As a young adult contemplating *Jesus Christ Superstar*, I am finding it hard to even start a conversation with my minister about it. But I continued to listen to this song about a thousand times across the next 40 years, and I quietly wonder what it must have been like to be Mary Magdalene. The lyrics indicate that there was some confusion between her eros love and philia love of Jesus. Is this true?

PSYCHOLOGICAL TOOL

Dr. James Fowler identified six stages of faith. Earlier in this chapter I described the first two stages. The third stage is called "Synthetic-Conventional Faith" which involves an older child broadening her scope beyond the influence of just the immediate family. She now pays attention to the media, peers, school and her community, and she needs to try to synthesize all these influences. At first she may tend to reject anything new that does not match up with the norms and conventions taught to her by her parents or other authority figures. But she shows signs of readiness for the next stage of faith when she experiences serious contradictions between credible authorities. This usually begins in adolescence and is a very unsettling time of life. She leaves the secure confidence of knowing exactly what she believes and now she questions what she has been taught. Fowler calls the fourth stage "Individuative-Reflective Faith" because she must reflect and then decide on her faith for herself as an individual, even if her family or friends disagree with her.[15]

Fowler had not written his book on the *Stages of Faith* until 1981, so I did not have the benefit of his description of my crisis-of-faith experience in the 1970's when *Godspell* and *Jesus Christ Superstar* were produced. I only knew that I had tremendous conflict and could not sort it out. I had to reconcile the contradiction, which meant that one of the identities attributed to Mary Magdalene had to be right and the other had to be a heresy. I felt that maybe the creators of these musical plays were not devoted Christians so they were probably just making fun of this sacred story. It must be blasphemy! But why were thousands of people going to see the show and listening to the songs? We didn't have an emperor's army available to charge down Broadway and stamp out the heretics and tell us the producers were blasphemous to create such a show. I suppose the Pope made some proclamations about it, but since I was not Catholic I didn't pay much attention to him. I was away from home and I don't know what the Christian clergy were saying about it all. I was in a private struggle to synthesize these conflicting identities of Mary Magdalene in terms of her relationship to Jesus Christ. This crisis got me started in my yearning to understand her. I had to figure it out, and I have been working on this puzzle for years.

PSYCHOLOGICAL TOOL

In the 1970's Dr. William Perry was at Harvard University studying the intellectual developmental stages that typical college students seem to go through when they are maturing from adolescence to adulthood. He was not focusing particularly on faith, but his theory can be applied to ethical and spiritual development. The theory states that younger college students assume that there are authorities who had all the answers to life's big questions and students just had to learn to memorize them. Later on, college students realize that some authorities are frauds and should be dismissed. Then students mature a bit and become aware of conflicting authorities, each with their valid points. It is not unusual for some older students to then distrust all authorities, and just rely on their own inner thoughts. Eventually, students have to make their first personal commitment to a creed and stick with it, even if they are attacked. Once they have done this the first time, they get used to making other public commitments to their individual

---

beliefs and gain confidence in their own ability to make important decisions. It is a sign of maturity when a college student can tolerate and even respect other people's creeds while being devoted to his or her own belief system. This maturation might not be completed during the college years.[16]

 As I consider Perry's theory, I understand that he is telling me that my journey was actually quite typical for a young adult. In my case the subject matter was my struggle with the two conflicting identities of Mary Magdalene. For my peers, it might have been a different subject: explaining war or death, for example. But Perry reassures us that this intellectual progression is quite normal and necessary. We need to shake off our assumption that we can just memorize what the authorities in our lives teach us. We must eventually think for ourselves.

Critics of Perry state that his description of this maturation process is more typical of men, especially since he mostly did his research on male college students at Harvard over 40 years ago. Since then other psychologists have described a different journey that adult women experience as they gradually learn to think for themselves.

In the next chapter, I will bring in a remarkable psychological tool to help us see how women seem to mature on their own unique pathway to understanding what it is that they think and believe. I will apply it to my own reflections about Mary Magdalene who was becoming my favorite role model.

CHAPTER 2

Are We Distracted By Her Sex Life?

People are curious about sex. No surprise. When we do not know the details of a famous actor's personal life, we might fill in the gaps with our imaginations. We might read about movie stars and royalty and wonder who is dating whom. We are falsely attributing things to them, and yet we might even convince ourselves that these things are true.

When we have fragments of evidence to encourage our imaginations we may leap to conclusions and think: "I knew it!" I am no different, although now I am making an effort to slow down my tendency to jump to conclusions about others. So what fragments of evidence do we have about Mary Magdalene and her personal relationship with Jesus? Let's examine the evidence closely so we can weed out these assumptions that people are making about her sex life.

I first heard that song from *Jesus Christ Superstar* decades ago, and I imagined that she was wondering about her own devotion to Jesus. The person who wrote those lyrics chose to portray her as confusing her spiritual devotion with a sexual attraction. As I struggle in my wondering about the truth regarding her relationship, I wanted some authority to just tell me what was correct, so I could stop debating. I wanted to settle the matter!

PSYCHOLOGICAL TOOL
In the 1980's, Dr. Mary Belenky, a developmental psychologist, led a group of other psychologists to carefully study how women know what they

know. They went beyond Perry's work about the cognitive development of adolescent college men. After careful interviews of women in many socio-economic groups and various ages, the psychologists came to the conclusion that there are many ways that women "know what they know", and women do not all go through a predictable set of stages in a sequential order completed by age 22. They seriously challenge Perry's work as not being generalizable to adult females. Belenky describes one of the seven frames of thinking as "Received Knowledge." When women focus on this way of knowing they see themselves as relying on outside authorities and referring to these experts to sound credible. They might start statements with "Well, I heard that . . . " or "The experts say . . . ." These women believe that truth comes from others who know much more than they do, and they doubt their own intuition. When asked what they think, they often say: "I don't know".[17]

During the beginning of my search process to find out about Mary Magdalene's sexual behavior, I was ready to just "Receive Knowledge" about her from the experts. I wanted to go to sources that were certainly more reliable than Tim Rice, who wrote the lyrics for the Broadway musical *Jesus Christ Superstar*. Where did he get that idea that her sexuality was a key part of her story? Was he the first to make that up? Did he do it so people would be more intrigued with the story?

Over the next few decades I started to see that there were two basic directions I needed to go in my search. One direction had to do with researching the identity of Mary Magdalene as a repentant prostitute/adulterer, and the other direction of my study was researching the identity of her as a loving companion of Jesus. Both involved her sexuality, which was a bit intriguing, but I still wondered if this part of her life even mattered. I feel such a fondness for Mary Magdalene that I sincerely hoped she had a committed sexual relationship with a man, but this aspect of her life just does not seem relevant to the essential Easter story. Was this excitement all just a distraction to pull everyone's attention away from something more important about her?

Where did the idea come from that Mary Magdalene was a sinner, specifically a sexual sinner, who later found Jesus and changed her ways? What authorities were the most credible? As Belenky describes, I was depending on Receiving Knowledge from experts.

As many people do, I started my search with simple books such as *The Everything Mary Magdalene Book*.[18] I knew it was a popularized source, but it seemed to be a quick way to get an answer. Then, of course, I tried Wikipedia.com and Google.com. At the time, I thought I could just get some simple answers and be done with solving this puzzle. I had too many other things to worry about in my career and family life to spend much time on this. I was very impatient, at first. But the answers were not simple, so I dug deeper. I went to the publications of modern, scholarly authorities who wrote books such as: *Mary Magdalen: Myth and Metaphor*,[19] *The Meaning of Mary Magdalene*,[20] and *Beloved Disciple*.[21]

To be honest, I was also having a few nagging doubts about the credibility of female scholars. I was raised in an environment that did not take females too seriously when it came to being experts on religion and Christian history, so I had to directly address my own lingering prejudice about women. I had so few role models of female religious scholars that I had to decide if these female authors were worth reading. I am a bit ashamed of this initial doubt, but this was all part of my process, so I share it with you. Gradually I changed this prejudiced view and grew in my respect for all of these scholars, regardless of their gender . . . more about this later.

So what was I finding as I dug through these written and visual accounts of Mary Magdalene's sex life? I saw dozens of paintings of her with her red hair, loose and long, often covering a partially nude, voluptuous body. Then I checked the *Holy Bible* focusing on the canonical Gospels again and could not find any passage that directly said Mary Magdalene was a prostitute or an adulterer. Why were these artists creating this identity of her? Was it just exciting and sexy to put her in this image? Was this the same as pornography to grab our attention on a sensual level and distract us away from something far more potent?

Then I learned that Pope Gregory the Great gave a certain sermon in 591 AD. Scholars claim that this Pope was the first to draw attention to her sexuality when he conflated the identities of Mary Magdalene and the following unnamed woman mentioned in the Holy Bible, into one combined persona:

 And there was a woman in the city who was a sinner; and when she learned that He was reclining at the table in the Pharisee's house, she brought an alabaster vial of perfume, and standing behind Him at His feet, weeping, she began to wet His feet with her tears, and kept wiping them with the hair of her head, and kissing His feet and anointing them with the perfume. Now when the Pharisee who had invited Him saw this, he said to himself, "If this man were a prophet He would know who and what sort of person this woman is who is touching Him, that she is a sinner." (*Holy Bible*: Luke 7: 37-39)

Pope Gregory stated:

She whom Luke calls the sinful woman, whom John calls Mary, we believe to be the Mary from whom seven devils were ejected according to Mark. And what did these seven devils signify, if not all the vices? . . . . It is clear, brothers, that the woman previously used the unguent to perfume her flesh acts.[22]

In Pope Gregory's homily he does say that she was a sinner as he combined this story of a woman with the other stories that mention Mary Magdalene. He does not actually say what her sin was. One scholar tells us that the Pope used the word peccatrix in his Latin sermon, which means sinner. If he had wanted to call her a prostitute he would have called her meretrix. He didn't.[23] He also emphasized in many sermons that she had a great love for Jesus. But the Pope did say the woman used a perfume for her flesh acts, which clearly refers to her sexuality. Confusing!

As time went by, other theologians kept referring to Pope Gregory's statement that she was a sinner and then they filled in the gaps. Then artists illustrated this image. They elaborated on this assertion in the Pope's homily and combined Mary Magdalene with characters from other dramatic Biblical stories that referred to sexual behavior, such as this one:

> But Jesus went to the Mount of Olives. At dawn he appeared again in the temple courts, where all the people gathered around him, and he sat down to teach them. The teachers of the law and the Pharisees brought in a woman caught in adultery. They made her stand before the group and said to Jesus, "Teacher, this woman was caught in the act of adultery. In the Law Moses commanded us to stone such women. Now what do you say?" They were using this question as a trap, in order to have a basis for accusing him. But Jesus bent down and started to write on the ground with his finger. When they kept on questioning him, he straightened up and said to them, "Let any one of you who is without sin be the first to throw a stone at her." Again he stooped down and wrote on the ground. At this, those who heard began to go away one at a time, the older ones first, until only Jesus was left, with the woman still standing there. Jesus straightened up and asked her, "Woman, where are they? Has no one condemned you?" "No one, sir," she said. "Then neither do I condemn you," Jesus declared. "Go now and leave your life of sin." (*Holy Bible*: John 8: 1-11)

This story from John does involve a woman who broke the commandment about sex outside of marriage, and it does describe how Jesus forgave her. But it does not say her name at all. No one currently knows who this woman was. In addition we have this specific reference to Mary Magdalene:

"When Jesus rose early on the first day of the week, he appeared first to Mary Magdalene, out of whom he had driven seven demons." (*Holy Bible*: Mark 16: 9)

What does this mean to have seven demons driven out of her? As a psychologist I have wondered about this for many years and not just when I am studying Mary Magdalene. What were these demons like and what did they cause people to do when they were inside the person, before being cast out? Notice that it does not actually say in the *Holy Bible* that she was doing anything sexually inappropriate when these seven demons were in possession of her body and mind. We are left to speculate.

Is there some place in the *Holy Bible* where we can get a clue about the nature of these seven demons? Some branches of the Christian faith hold the books of Proverbs and Epistle to the Galatians to be divine authorities on the same level as the four canonical Gospels: Matthew, Mark, Luke and John. While I am aware that these books are very important to some people, I respectfully disagree. I do not consider them to be divine or at the same level of importance as the canonical Gospels, but I view them more as Christian historical documents. As a result, I question their validity.

In the books of Proverbs and Epistle to the Galatians there are references to the seven deadly sins, which include lust. This list of serious sins has changed over the last 200 years but lust is usually on the list of things NOT to do. Yet it is a leap to say that the seven demons cast out of Mary Magdalene (mentioned in the Gospel of Mark) were the same as the list of seven deadly sins (mentioned in these non-Gospel books). How can I sort this out? There are so many loose threads being tied together: can I untangle them?

THEOLOGICAL TOOL

Emanuel Swedenborg is the theologian who offers such a compelling argument for reading the Bible less literally and more interiorly. He provides an interpretation of the *Holy Bible* and explains about the demons that possessed people, and yet he

---

never mentions the seven deadly sins at all. He states: "Spirits who do not unite with our thoughts . . . enter our bodies and take over all its senses, talking through our mouths and acting through our limbs. It seems to them entirely as though every-thing of ours were theirs. These are the spirits that possess people; but they have been cast into hell by the Lord and moved decisively away; so possession like this no longer occurs nowadays". He also says: "The demons cast out by the Lord, by which many were then obsessed, signify falsities of every kind by which the church was infested, and from which it was then delivered by the Lord". In addition, Swedenborg indicates that the number seven corresponds to the concept of completeness, thus Mary Magdalene might have felt totally consumed by these falsifying demons until Jesus cast them out. However, he also indicates that seven represents what is holy and inviolable. The internal sense of these seven demons possessing her means that she may have felt completely con-sumed by evil words and behaviors, but her inner thoughts and spirit were actually never violated.[24]

 Swedenborg teaches an alternative view of the idea of demon possession. If I use this per-spective I do not have to focus on her sexual behavior. The demons that were temporarily residing in her correspond to false ideas that had infiltrated the church at that time, and Jesus Christ had the power to cast them out. This might not have anything to do with her sexuality. I think of the seven demons possessing her as closer to a kind of mental illness such as schizophrenia in which she might hear voices urging her to do odd things. While demons may have taken over her words and behavior, leading her to do all kinds of destructive actions, still her inner soul was untouched. It is possible that she had been sexually active or even exploited while under the influence of these demons. However, I do not think she was completely respon-sible for her actions until the demons left her mind and body. Imagine Mary Magdalene being freed of that mental difficulty when Jesus performed this miracle. Once that occurred, her

spiritual regeneration could begin. Then she could decide for herself whether to be sexually involved in a relationship. Before that, it was not her choice.

MARY MAGDALENE IS POSSESSED BY SEVEN DEMONS
PAINTING BY WERNER

MARY MAGDALENE IS SERENE AFTER DEMONS WERE CAST OUT
PAINTING BY WERNER

MARY MAGDALENE, PAINTING BY NICOT
TROYES, FRANCE

The psychologist Mary Belenky would probably describe me as Receiving Knowledge from all these sources: canonical Gospels in the *Holy Bible*, Christian history books included in the *Holy Bible*, sermons from a Catholic Pope, and Swedenborg's interpretations of the Gospels of the *Holy Bible*. By now I was starting to prioritize ideas according to which sources I found to be the most credible, so I was not just passively Receiving Knowledge anymore. I was much more engaged and critical of what I was reading.

I could see now that Roman Catholic theologians, in the 600 years after Mary Magdalene lived, started conflating this story in John of the adulterous woman with the story in Luke about the woman with the alabaster jar and with the specific stories of Mary Magdalene with her demons. Then artists of paintings and stained glass in the medieval era of Europe were commissioned to illustrate this combined image. Mary's identity was solidified and remained in people's minds for the next 1400 years. The Protestant and Roman Catholic churches of the 16th to the 20th centuries were still holding onto this perspective that she was a repentant adulterer or prostitute after a thousand years. Few seemed to question it. The church leaders built an entire system of institutions based on this mistaken assumption, and they perpetuated this myth. Mary Magdalene was made the patron saint of fallen women. There is both a condemnation and a celebration of her repentance. I wonder about their assumption that she had spiritual freedom during the time of her possession when she was an alleged fallen woman. I conclude that her inner spirit was protected and inviolable, and yet her freedom of choice was temporarily clouded over by these demons. Once the demons were cast out, then she was capable of acting purposefully. So I prefer to think of her as mostly consumed by these evil spirits against her will, but then set free when He cast them out. This represents how we can ask the Lord for His help as we get entrapped in false ideas and evil behaviors, and He is always ready to help us. We are only responsible for what we do out of free will, and especially if we love to do it.

As part of my research I watched a modern movie called *The Magdalen Sisters*.[25] It is based on first hand accounts of girls who escaped from the Magdalen Asylums and Laundries. These Catholic residences were built in many countries where Christianity was spreading, but they were the most common in England and Ireland. According to historians, Catholic girls who had been either willingly sexually active or unwilling victims of sexual abuse were all rejected and sent to these Christian reformatories. In this subculture sex was considered profane, so these girls were captured and sent away by their parents and local priests.

If there was a pregnancy involved, the girl stayed until the baby was born and sold to an adopting family. Some girls stayed there the rest of their lives because they had nowhere else to go. Their families were ashamed of their sexual behaviors and few men would marry women with such damaged reputations. The nuns of these institutions supervised the residents, calling them children regardless of their ages. The residents were also nicknamed "Maggies" or "Magdalens" and they were treated like slaves. The lives of the Maggies in these institutions consisted of managing the laundry and sewing for the people in the nearby mansions. The nuns kept all the income generated from this work. Maggies were not educated or trained for any other profession. In addition to spending their days in mute slave labor, the Maggies were required to pray for forgiveness for their sexual sins and model their lives after their repentant saint, Mary Magdalene.[26]

I feel furious about this oppression of girls and women as well as this portrayal of Mary Magdalene with a focus on her alleged sex life. For centuries these Maggies had no political power to change this system, and certainly no voice in such a punishing, patriarchal church institution. They were definitely not encouraged to question authority or investigate the true story about the meaning of demon possession of their patron saint. In addition, these enslaving institutions named after Mary Magdalene seem far removed from the message of compassion and forgiveness advocated by Jesus when he talked to the woman found in adultery. They were based on distaste for sexuality, confusion about Mary Magdalene's freedom of choice, and domination over females.

PSYCHOLOGICAL TOOL

Dr. Nancy Downing, a social psychologist, analyzed some stages that people seem to go through after they have been oppressed and denied their civil rights. She asserts that at first people are very subdued about their oppressed status in life. In the initial stage of "Passive Acceptance", people trust their authority figures. However, then they have an awakening and think: "Wait a second . . . this can't be right!" Downing calls this stage "Revelation". Then downtrodden people mistrust their oppressors and authoritarian leaders. A natural reaction to this is for these oppressed people to try to flee and then gather together to discuss the abuse, in their "Embeddedness" stage. They compare notes on what was happening and plan a rebellion. After a while, some people may try to make social changes so this kind of abuse does not occur again, which is their "Active Commitment" stage. Downing applies this theory when she analyzes the psychological progression happening to former slaves, people who could not vote, or victims of any violence.[27]

Downing's theory can help us explain what it is like for anyone who has been neglected, abused or oppressed. This stage theory helps me to understand what it must have been like for these women to be sexually abused, rejected by society and then sent to the Magdalene Laundries as slaves. Although the Maggies were given a message of hope through repentance, there was not a chance for most of these 30,000 girls and women to re-enter society after paying for their sins through years of hard labor. Most of them were probably stuck in the lower psychological stages of "Passive Acceptance" and "Revelation", because there was no way to escape. Using Downing's theory as a lens, I can see that some of these women may have felt accepting of their lot as they prayed to Mary Magdalene, while some others may have been extremely angry, especially if they had been raped and then harshly punished by the nuns and priests. Some eyewitnesses claim that the Maggies were often raped by the very people who were supposed to be their guardians: the clergymen. How ironic.

The last institution of this type closed its doors in 1996 and investigators are finding physical evidence to support the Maggies' claims. When the girls and women ran away they told the media of their ordeal. A book and a movie were produced in 2003. We are living in the first generation of women who exposed this horrific organization, which had been run by Christian leaders. Downing's theory helps us see the social progression of these "Maggies" as a group across hundreds of years: from their initial "Passive Acceptance"; then "Revelation" and rebellion against the oppression; then "Embeddedness" while women were comparing notes with other women who had been oppressed; and finally "Active Commitment" when they were working to make social changes by telling the story. Now advocates are bringing this to the world's attention through investigations and the media. I am grateful that this institutionalized abuse has come to an end.

Not every church organization promoted this persona of Mary Magdalene as their justification for oppressing women. It feels reassuring to see that the leaders of the Eastern Orthodox Church never agreed with the Roman Catholic theologians in this combined portrayal of Mary Magdalene. They consistently dismissed any reference to her sexual behavior and certainly never ran any Magdalen Laundries. I agree with their position and am grateful to them for having the courage to stand up to the widespread Roman Catholic Church for hundreds of years. I imagine that this was difficult.

And now I find it remarkable that in 1969, the Roman Catholic Church quietly changed its stance about Mary Magdalene in their Missal (Biblical readings, rituals and calendar). In effect, they told their parishioners to read about Mary

Magdalene as she is portrayed on Easter morning in the canonical Gospels, and they no longer call her "Mary Magdalene, penitent." They were un-doing the work of Pope Gregory after 1378 years. I can find nothing in writing about this huge Vatican announcement for change, occurring back in 1969. No big announcement happened! This policy change was discovered by Catholic scholars who were searching for the essential Mary Magdalene, just like I am, and they released this quiet development to the popular press several years after 1969. So, in the first decade of the 21st century, dozens of books have been published describing this sequence of events and we can each evaluate what happened to the Catholic Church's position about Mary Magdalene.[28]

Just because a person has positional authority such as being a Pope does not mean that he can't be mistaken. I realize they have the tradition of calling the Pope infallible, but this is clearly an example of human error. I only wish the modern day Vatican spokesmen had the courage to admit their errors more publicly. So many women were harmed in the name of theology, and so was the legacy of Mary Magdalene. I am still waiting for the day when the current Pope apologizes to the Maggies.

THEOLOGICAL TOOL
Swedenborg provides us with interpretations of the stories in the *Holy Bible*. In addition, he also describes how power has been terribly abused by some of the leaders of the organized Christian churches. He explains how individual church leaders will be judged when they die and go to the afterlife. Swedenborg states that it will not matter what official rank the church leaders held in this world. What matters is what they understood to be true, what they loved to do, and whether they genuinely cared about the effects they had on other people. Swedenborg teaches us that we will all go through such a judgment as our ruling loves become clear. The more sincerely we love what is good, seek what is true, and then willingly strive to live a useful life, the more we are seeking eternal life

in heaven. Those leaders who sincerely tried to serve their parishioners will be separated from those that just loved to dominate them.[29]

 Applying this Swedenborgian perspective I can see that perhaps the Maggies were being taught to be useful and remorseful, but it was taken to an extreme. The girls and women were there against their will and forced into a life of painful labor and prayer. Some may have previously been sexually promiscuous by choice and some may have been victims of incest or rape. The church leaders did not take this distinction into account. They only looked at the girls' sexual behavior, not their intentions. The leaders only blamed the women, not the men, who were engaged in these sexual acts. Swedenborg teaches us that in the afterlife all church leaders, the Maggies, and the men in their sexual lives will be reviewed individually for the sincerity of their motives. Justice will finally prevail.

I find great comfort in this perspective, to calm my outrage at the way these girls were treated by misogynous church leaders. I believe in an afterlife, and this description offered by Swedenborg helps me trust that there is some kind of fairness in providence. I also buy into the Swedenborgian view that sexuality is a wonderful gift from the Lord and should not be viewed with disgust. Adolescent girls are not usually mature enough to handle their potent sexuality, so they need gentle guidance rather than condemnation as they gradually learn to handle this gift. It is not until they reach a mature age of reason (in adulthood) that they are truly responsible for their sexual decisions. The Lord is very forgiving and holds out hope that everyone will eventually choose to establish a committed, sexual union with a beloved partner. The Lord pays attention to both our reasoning and our will.

At this point in my journey of studying Mary Magdalene from multiple perspectives, I was starting to trust my own ways of analyzing these stories and not just passively receiving everything I knew from experts. I was consulting experts but also trusting my intuition. This led me to ponder many ways of knowing the stories about Mary Magdalene.

PSYCHOLOGICAL TOOL
Dr. Belenky and other psychologists identified at least a half dozen ways women know what they know. In addition to the common pattern of women just using their "Received Knowledge" from authorities in a passive manner, women also have "Subjective Knowledge," "Procedural Knowledge" and "Constructed Knowledge." When women have more freedom, rights and respect they are more likely to use these other ways of knowing. "Subjective Knowing" includes an increased trust in their own intuition, especially after encountering unfair authority figures. Belenky describes two specific patterns of "Subjective Knowing", which she calls "The Quest for Self" and "The Inner Voice".[30]

In addition to Receiving Knowledge, I question some authorities and balance what they teach me against my own intuitive ideas. Now I am more doubtful of some of the leaders in the Roman Catholic Church who combine Mary Magdalene's identity with other women in the Gospel stories. Through their mighty influence they had successfully directed the attention of millions of their church members away from her key role on Easter morning to this scandalous story of her sexual behavior. They directed artists to portray her in this manner. They wrote sermons and distributed them across the globe, and they condemned sexually active women to a life of slave labor and called them Maggies. Because Jesus had cast out seven demons from Mary Magdalene's life, the Roman Catholic clergy assumed this meant that she had willfully sinned and then repented from her promiscuous life.

My outrage had fueled me to move beyond Passive Acceptance of these messages, even if they came from people in high-ranking positions. I feel fortunate to live in a place and time when women can question religious authorities and not be burned at the stake, figuratively or literally! So I enhanced my search and explored my own "Inner Voice." I went inside and examined my intrapersonal life in my "Quest for Self." I discovered that I needed a role model as I was figuring out whom I was becoming.

PHILOSOPHICAL TOOL

Dr. Harry Moody is a modern day philosopher who is fascinated with the spiritual journey that many men and women experience. He interviews hundreds of elderly people and offers a theory of the most common stages of spiritual life. He does not advocate any one particular theological position, but he does see common stages that people seem to experience. He acknowledges that not every person goes through all these stages in perfect order or even progresses to the final stage, but he offers this description to help spiritual seekers understand their own pathways. He describes the *Five Stages of the Soul* as: 1) the Call, 2) the Search, 3) the Struggle, 4) the Breakthrough, and 5) the Return.[31]

Belenky and Moody both teach us that it is normal to experience a difficult spiritual journey. Belenky, the psychologist, calls it the "Subjective Knowledge: Quest for Self" while Moody, the philosopher, calls it the stages of the "Call, Search and Struggle". I find it reassuring to hear their names of stages for my experiences. I am not feeling condemned for questioning authorities as I try to figure out who I am spiritually. It is a challenging journey, but through this process I am gradually learning to trust my intuition and feminine perception.

Although I am not exactly the same as the Maggies who prayed to their repentant patron saint, I am similar in that I do need to understand Mary Magdalene's life and then use her as a role model. So my troublesome search for the essential Mary Magdalene is also part of my personal quest for spiritual growth.

At the beginning of this chapter I indicated that there are

two areas that I need to investigate about the sexual life of Mary Magdalene. I have just summarized how Mary Magdalene was misapprehended as a possessed and willfully, sexually promiscuous woman who later repented. I feel increasingly certain that I can sort through these tales and dismiss the ones my intuition does not accept. I can challenge church leaders and am beginning to forgive them for blemishing her character during all these centuries. It is not my job to condemn them, but I do respectfully disagree with what they have done to her persona.

The second area of her sexual life that I am investigating is the assertion that she was a very close partner of Jesus Christ. Just as I can recall the incident when I first heard Mary Magdalene's song from *Jesus Christ Superstar*, I can remember exactly where I was when I first became aware of Dan Brown's novel, *The DaVinci Code*.[32] The mystery-detective novel was first published in 2003 and was becoming a bestseller.

I recall the day that I was driving along in my car during a very boring commute. I drive long distances between my home and workplace, so I listen to novels on tapes and CD's as a way to pass the time. No one had told me the details of the plot, so I was clueless when I acquired this novel and played it for entertainment. Brown is a gifted writer. As I listened and drove I was totally engaged in the twists of the plot and the exciting chase of the characters across Europe. The hours flew by. But then when the author got to the part of the story where one of the novel's characters explained that Jesus was married to Mary Magdalene and that she was pregnant with His child at the time of his crucifixion . . . I had to put on the brakes. I stopped the car, got out and started pacing energetically around the highway rest area.

I was flabbergasted! I couldn't believe my ears. How could he say such a thing? I got back in the car and replayed this part again and again. When I finally got home, I pulled out my old art history books and looked for a copy of the painting by DaVinci illustrating the Last Supper. Brown is claiming that this was an image that included a pregnant Mary Magdalene next to Jesus Christ, not one of the younger, beardless male disciples as most of us assume. I wondered. Could it possibly be true? Why didn't I ever hear this from the clergy of my church? Marriage is highly valued by my branch of Christianity, so maybe it would be lovely to think of Jesus and Mary as married role models. But wait — the clergy told me that the sacred marriage is God with His Church. Many Christian sects promote this concept. Should Mary represent all of us in His church?

Since I had a growing confidence in my ability to sort through Brown's version of the life of Mary Magdalene, I quickly started going into a critique. Was this just an historical novel in which the author builds an invented story around a few documented facts? Was he the first person to ever make such an assertion? It was certainly the first time I had ever heard this claim, but just because it was a first for me does not mean that the idea wasn't around before 2003. But it took this best-selling novel and movie to get my attention about this concept. Apparently it also got the attention of millions of others across the globe. This novel is continually promoted by the media and is very hard to ignore. Many people seem to swallow the story whole. I have heard people say they distrust all church leaders, and Brown portrays the Vatican as covering up the story of this marriage. I can completely understand these people's distrust of some church leaders, but I am not agreeing with Brown's tale. This novel is fueling the fires of an enormous debate.[33]

Indignant Roman Catholic historians are protesting *The DaVinci Code* in earnest and urging Catholics to boycott the book and movie. This novel flew in the face of the Catholic assumption that Jesus was celibate. Catholics require their male clergy to follow in His footsteps and denounce their earthly, sexual urges for their higher love of God.

Now theological and historical scholars are challenging the facts mentioned in Brown's novel. He was even taken to court about the quality of his research and whether he had borrowed too much from a previous publication called *Holy Blood, Holy Grail*.[34] On the one hand he claims to have invented the concept of the marriage of Jesus and Mary Magdalene, but on the other hand he claims that it is a secret idea that has been around for centuries. His inconsistency only makes investigators dig deeper. In public, he often hides behind his right as a novelist to spin any tale he likes, regardless of the consequences.

So I began buying current books about Mary Magdalene, lots of them. It seems that this idea of Mary Magdalene's sexual union with Jesus was previously promoted by the Mormons, the Masons, and even the Nazis of Germany! This was news to me. Another best-selling novelist of historical fiction is Kathleen McGowan.[35] In her recent publications she also claims that Mary Magdalene and Jesus were married and had a few children. Like Brown, McGowan writes such exciting stories that it is easy to get swept up into the concept of Mary's special pregnancy. But it is important for me to peel away the fantasies from the truth.

In the first couple of years of my research I read several of these stories and yet I put a moratorium on coming to any hurried conclusion about this assertion of their marriage and child. Now I look at the premise of these novels more critically and try to stand back a bit to keep my imagination from getting away from me. After I finish each of these novels, I go inward and reflect and wonder. What does my intuition say about this incredible idea? Could there have been a bloodline of descendants of Mary and Jesus? I go back and forth between consulting my own intuition and reliable resources.

Dr. Sharan Newman is the author of one of my favorite resources that I recently discovered.[36] She is a scholar who provides a practical encyclopedia of terms, rituals, characters and ideas in plain English. I read it so that I can balance this information against Brown's compelling story and the persuasive arguments of the irate people at the Vatican. It is becoming a three-way debate in my mind.

An especially troubling part of the storyline in both McGowan's and Brown's novels is their claim that at least one child of Mary Magdalene and Jesus Christ was born and raised in France. McGowan and Brown explain that the descendants of this bloodline became important people in the following centuries. These descendants were supposedly persecuted and threatened by the Roman Catholic Church to keep this information quiet, so secret societies were formed to protect details from the public. People in these secret organizations felt they were quite special, so they established rituals and codes for transferring this vital information to later generations while avoiding the wrath of the organized church. McGowan and Brown use their novels to tell us that both men and women were allowed to be leaders in these secret societies, which is also in contrast to the traditional practice of a male only clergy. I can see how this detail alone is also a bone of contention with the many Catholic Church leaders.

With all these debates swirling in my mind, I frequently pulled away from my reading and the influence of others to consider what I really thought about it all. I meditated on my understanding of God, His relationship with the churches on earth, and reflected on my own beliefs. I started using my discernment to peel away the distracting stories that I viewed as false. I prayed and listened to a still small voice from within. I wondered if I would ever get clarity. I reflected on whether the supposed descendants of this couple claim to have any extra advantage about getting into heaven? How do the rest of us earn eternal life if we do not happen to be descendants of Jesus and Mary Magdalene?

 Around the same time that Brown published his detective-novel in 2003, I also became aware of research about the important role of Mary Magdalene as described in newly discovered, ancient documents. These seemed to be more credible than what was written by the modern novelist who was making a fortune off of his fanciful tale. I had not previously paid much attention to this area, but when I heard that Mary Magdalene's special relationship to Jesus was mentioned in writings from over 1700 years ago I just had to investigate.

I discovered that in the first three centuries A.D. there were many types of Christians, each striving to live according to the teachings of Christ. I am not an historian, so I have to venture into this area as a novice. I certainly cannot translate the recently discovered ancient documents, so I have to depend on the expertise of translators, theologians and historians. But I am still free to decide for myself if the written ideas have any validity, even if they are hundreds of years old.

I am particularly struck by the discovery of *The Gospel of Mary*. This is a fragmented document that was found in 1896 in Egypt, and smaller fragments of copies of this same Gospel are being discovered. Apparently, when historians find additional copies of the same document, this confirms the validity in their minds.[37]

In this remarkable document there is a story that tells us that Mary was talking to the other apostles after Jesus had risen. She has heard His message through her inner voice (called "nous") and is now conveying these ideas to the others. She comforts them when they are frightened and tells them to remember to spread the news of the resurrection. The male apostles are conflicted. Should they listen to a woman, who is not even allowed to be a legal witness in their culture? Yet they all knew she was loved by Jesus more than all the others, so maybe they should believe her declarations of hearing Him through her meditations and intuition. After all, she was His favorite and asked to be His witness.

Another document found at the same Egyptian location also describes the relationship of Jesus and Mary. This *Gospel of Philip* is mostly about the process of spiritual initiation. But there is one intriguing section: a part of a sentence indicates that Jesus loves Mary and "kisses her on the _____." The document is broken here, so we can only guess. Since this document was found, people have wondered if he kisses her on the mouth as a sign of a special sexual relationship. Yet, in other parts of this same document it indicates that kissing was a means of receiving grace and spreading peace between believers, and not just a sign of sexuality. In the text of the *Gospel of Philip* the apostles are asking why He kisses her. But if Jesus and Mary Magdalene were actually married, why would the apostles even question Him kissing her? There is nothing in these documents that says that they were married or had a child between them. That is all speculation. I believe, as the Greeks would say, that she had a philia type of love for Him and He had an agape type of love for her, not eros love.

In my personal reflection I think that it is more probable that Mary was just a devoted follower and apostle spreading the good news to others. She appears to have had her spiritual eyes and ears open to be receptive to His wisdom, even after He rose from the dead. Some of the early Christians must have loved this way of learning about the truth, as they also practiced meditation and listening from within. They longed for Jesus to visit them in their minds. Many called this group of Christians "Gnostics", or people who knew. Apparently Gnostics felt like the Holy Spirit had filled them because they claimed to have a deeper understanding of the truth. They seemed to want to be like Mary Magdalene who had such a rich comprehension and pure heart that Jesus frequently visited her spirit during her meditations.[38]

At this time the various people who were called Gnostics were pulling away from the political authorities of the Roman Empire, the Jewish Rabbis and any Christian leaders who claimed to be ordained by the apostles. The Gnostics had more faith in their inner voices and private spiritual searches than in these leaders. Some of the Gnostics wrote down their inner knowledge and then secretly stored these documents in containers in the desert. They also combined their own inner knowledge with ideas from even more ancient cultures, so that it is often hard to tell these Christian ideas apart from fantasies or Greek concepts. Their Gospels were not consistent. Gnostic people varied quite a bit in their views about Jesus Christ: was he Divine or Human? It is understandable that opinions might vary on this issue, since it is quite complicated. People still ponder this question today.

Apparently the early Christian Church was getting organized about the time of the Council of Nicea in 321 AD. With the emperor at the helm, political might reinforced the decisions of this Christian council. The newly formed Catholic Church leaders determined that they were ordained in a sequence since Peter and Paul so they were the true apostolic church, and they thought most of the Gnostics were just heretics. The ordained clergy claimed that the Gnostics had taken the thoughts from their inner voices, mixed them with elaborate fantasies and then promoted blasphemies as if they were the real truth. This meant that the gospels of Mary and Philip were considered a threat to the organized church. As a result, many documents were written, copied and then hidden from the Catholic Church leaders in secure containers, deep in the sand for 1700 years.[39]

Now, hundreds of documents are being discovered in Israel and Egypt after being stored underground or in caves. (I have seen the Dead Sea Scrolls that people claim are over 2000 years old!) Although it took decades for them to be carefully translated, preserved and made available to us in museums and published works, now we can read them. During this modern era we are much more politically and religiously free. Thus we can each use our intuition while we read, reflect, compare, contrast and then decide what we believe to be true about Jesus and Mary Magdalene.

THEOLOGICAL TOOL
Swedenborg describes how we are to make our own decisions in freedom according to reason. He claims that now it is permitted to enter intellectually into the mysteries of faith. No longer are adults to just be child-like followers of organized church leaders or any other persuasive element. By the time we are mature and of sound mind, we have the capacity and responsibility to use our rational minds to let go of any faith borrowed from our parents and to consider what we individually believe.[40]

Based on my investigation of these fantastic sexual stories of Mary Magdalene being either a reformed prostitute or the bride of Jesus, I am reflecting on what I consider to be true. At this time, I do not accept those distracting stories about her sex life as they pull our attention away from the important story. I see her as a wise and compassionate woman. I think she experienced a philia type of love for Jesus Christ and felt a thelema type of love for his ministry. I also hope she experienced a terrific eros type of love in a committed sexual marriage, but I don't think this is relevant to the Easter story.

She was brave in the face of danger and comforted other believers. I admire her because she did not seem to give credit to herself in any way and never promoted herself as superior to others. I love her apparent perception, her wisdom and her humility. I am peeling away the irrelevant falsities about her life and finding my role model.

Mary Magdalene at the cross, France

CHAPTER 3

A New Perspective
On Mary Magdalene.

A few years ago, I decided to join a group tour to see the stained glass windows of France. We were focusing on the beautifully pre-served windows in about twenty cathedrals built around the 12th century. One afternoon in the Vezalay Abbey in Burgundy, while we are straining our necks and eyes to look way up high to see the architecture and windows, I relax my gaze for a moment but keep listening to our tour guide. I stroll away from the group and come upon a sign near a staircase that says: "Basilique Ste-Madeleine." Madeleine . . . is this the same name as Magdalene?

I gather some pamphlets and let my friends know that I am going to explore. I discover an underground crypt with a chapel devoted to Mary Magdalene. Then I see candles and chairs facing the front of the chapel, where a gold container holds a tiny sliver of a bone. The signs tell me that this is a bone from the skull of Mary Magdalene: it is a relic and I real-ize that I have never been this close to one before! The sign says: "Reliques de Ste. Marie Madeleine."

I make some inquiries and learn that there are at least three places that claim to have her bones, cartilage, hair or even bits of skin. In Provence, France, there is a place called Saint-Maximin-la-Sainte-Baume where the monks still believe that they have her entire skull. It appears that there is a long complex history of the competition between the clergy in Vezalay and Provence. In addition, there is a cathedral in Israel that claims to have some of her relics that draw pilgrims to worship her.[41]

Starting nearly a thousand years ago, people yearned to be close to Mary Magdalene so they would walk on long pilgrimages to see these relics. Pilgrims still make this journey, and they make donations and pray that she will intervene and perform miracles in their lives. This increases the political and economic power of the religious leaders at those sites, so there is an enormous incentive to convince the pilgrims that these relics are authentic, mystical and magical. Thousands, maybe millions, of people believe in them, but I do not.

MARY MAGDALENE'S RELICS IN A CRYPT
VEZALAY, FRANCE

CATHEDRAL, PAINTING BY WERNER
BEUNE, FRANCE

CRUCIFIXION AND EASTER STORY
FRANCE

PSYCHOLOGICAL TOOL

Dr. Mary Belenky and other developmental psychologists investigate the ways that women think and understand. In earlier chapters we reviewed two ways: "Received Knowledge" and "Subjective Knowledge." Belenky also describes "Procedural Knowledge" and explains that there are two complementary kinds: "Procedural: Separate Knowing" and "Procedural: Connected Knowing." The separate type of knowing involves doubting, critical analysis and a willingness to pull away from other people and learn about ideas in an impersonal manner. This type of thinking is more traditionally conducted by men, especially well-trained male scientists and lawyers. However, thoughtful women can also experience this type of learning about the world. In contrast, the Connected type of knowing is based on a system of using procedures for gaining access to others' knowledge. This includes empathy for other people's perspectives.[42]

While praying quietly in this crypt, I am doubting the validity of these relics of Mary Magdalene. Belenky would say that I was exercising my "Separate Knowing" as I stand there in the candlelit Basilique Ste-Madeleine. I see other people who are devoted worshippers in sincere prayer as they earnestly hope she will intervene in their lives and bring them grace. I think of all the millions of people who are coming to this site, by foot or by tour bus, seeking spiritual transformation. I see modern day pilgrims wearing the ancient symbol of the scallop shell on their hats and jackets. This sign immediately communicates to others that they are on a spiritual pilgrimage, walking across Europe to visit the cathedrals and sites of these relics of saints. I was with the pilgrims, but also not with them. I knew I was separate because we have different ways of worshipping. I honor and respect their spiritual journeys but I do not share their devotion to these relics.

In that moment in the sacred space dedicated to Mary Magdalene, I feel more like an observer than a participant in the worship of Mary Magdalene's bone relic. I stay quiet near the pilgrims, but I keep myself off to the side of the crypt. I am actually feeling a bit envious of their intensity, but I just cannot bring myself to get down on my knees to worship her bone. This spiritual practice seems misguided and invented by the clergy. Where does the *Holy Bible* instruct us to worship saints and their bones?

A week later on this same tour of medieval cathedrals, I am dozing on the bus as I am a bit weary of all this traveling. I am not paying much attention to the plan for the day when the bus comes to a stop. I hear the guide say that we are arriving at Chartres Cathedral, so I perk up. I gather my gear and head for this marvelous cathedral. I think I have read about this place in my art history class decades ago. Isn't this where there are two unmatched towers? Yes, there they are; I can see them!

CHARTRES CATHEDRAL, PAINTING BY WERNER
FRANCE

LABYRINTH DESIGN ON FLOOR OF CHARTRES CATHEDRAL
FRANCE.

When I step inside Chartres Cathedral with my group, I notice that there are people slowly moving within a huge circle. They stop occasionally, and then solemnly close their eyes. Then I look at the stone floor. There, inserted in the stonework, is a labyrinth! This is a circular pathway that invites pilgrims and visitors to perform the spiritual practice of walking in a meditative manner, each with their own private thoughts. I had no idea I would see this here. At first I maintain my distant position as an observer, but then something compels me to step in. I take off my shoes and begin the slow walk, around the outer circle, back and forth on concentric lines, finally getting to the middle. One of my friends from our tour group also joins our labyrinth walk. We quietly acknowledge each other as we pass. I sense that I am slowly proceeding along parallel, curvy lines gradually getting to the outside circle of the labyrinth path, stopping occasionally, and meditating until the person in front of me moves again.

There are probably fifty of us, each lost in our inner thoughts and prayers. No one speaks a word and strangers rarely make eye contact even though we are often inches away from each other. No one is in charge of managing this crowd, but it is incredibly orderly, peaceful and serene. I have no idea how long it took to participate in this spiritual ritual but I have relived it a dozen times in my mind since then. Time does not matter in this spiritual event. I am delighted that within one week I am switching from the role of separate observer to the role of involved participant by simply removing my shoes and quietly following the pilgrim in front of me on the labyrinth at Chartres Cathedral.

I have since learned that the novelist, Kathleen McGowan, uses this experience of walking the labyrinth at Chartres as a centerpiece to her novel of historical fiction: *The Book of Love*. It is her assertion that the labyrinth was originally a pagan symbol that refers to the ancient myth of getting lost in a maze and arriving at the center to fight one's personal monsters. The myth implies that it is very hard to get out of such a labyrinth unscathed.

McGowan also tells the tale that Solomon built his temple

in Jerusalem to include such a labyrinth and then these architectural plans were handed down to Jesus and Mary Magdalene. Although there is almost nothing left of Solomon's destroyed temple to provide physical evidence to support her story, McGowan still claims that Jesus and Mary Magdalene adopted the labyrinth after Solomon, and made it into a Christian practice. McGowan also claims that the apostles of Jesus changed the labyrinth to include a cross through the middle, referring to His crucifixion. McGowan claims that this tale is supposed to be written in the actual non-canonical Gospel called the *Book of Love* that was found just long enough during the medieval time period to help architects design the labyrinth at Chartres Cathedral. She tells us that this alleged document was found but is now lost. She has created her historical fiction novel of the same name, *The Book of Love*.[44]

Back at Chartres Cathedral, I learn that this 42 foot wide labyrinth has eleven circuits that lead to the six-petaled rose in the center. In the Christian version of the ancient myth, we are encouraged to recite the Lord's Prayer while standing in the center on the stones shaped like a rose. McGowan feels that praying is another form of fighting our evil inner monsters, so there is a similarity to the ancient labyrinth tradition of having a spiritual experience in the center.

She divides the Lord's Prayer into six sections and calls them: 1) Faith, 2) Surrender, 3) Service, 4) Abundance, 5) Forgiveness, and 6) Strength. She argues that the phrases of the Lord's Prayer follow these themes, and a pilgrim should step on each of the six central petals while contemplating that particular part of the prayer. McGowan supports her assertions that this is all linked to words from Jesus and Mary Magdalene because there is a stained glass window of Mary Magdalene right near the entrance to the labyrinth at Chartres Cathedral.[45]

I had not yet read McGowan's book when I was visiting Chartres a few years ago. But I agree with her in that I love privately praying while I am walking the labyrinth along with other pilgrims. It is a serene moment while I engage in my walk. However, when I read her novel later on, I questioned

McGowan's evidence to support her assertions. I find no credible proof of the existence of an ancient document that she names the *Book of Love*, allegedly written by Jesus and Mary Magdalene.

According to the authorities at the Israel Museum in Jerusalem, there is no physical evidence of any labyrinth in the floor of the Solomon's temple, so this tale appears to be part of McGowan's fictional account. Yet I share McGowan's wonder about the mystery of why the architects of Chartres built one into the stone floor. There is nothing in the canonical Gospels directing architects to do this. Why did they do it? What is the link between the pre-Christian labyrinth myth and this Christian cathedral?[46]

McGowan offers a solution, as she focuses on the window of Chartres that is illustrating the story of Mary Magdalene. It is colorful and intriguing but it is still based on misconceptions from Pope Gregory about her being the same as the unnamed sinning woman who washes the feet of Jesus. So I disagree with McGowan's enthusiasm about the content of that window, and remain unconvinced that the location of this stained glass window is near the labyrinth's entrance for a reason. I think it is sheer coincidence. In conclusion, McGowan wrote a literary fantasy that is as fun to read as Brown's novel, *The DaVinci Code*, but I need to sort out the history from the fiction.

UNNAMED WOMAN WASHING THE FEET OF JESUS, CHARTRES CATHEDRAL
FRANCE

Belenky (the psychologist who focuses on female wisdom) emphasizes the worth of both Separate and Connected ways of women knowing what they know. Each way involves some intentional effort on my part when I think about Mary Magdalene. When I am conscious of my Separate understanding, I am feeling more doubtful, unconvinced of stories, and autonomous from those around me. I have to make a real effort not to be too loud and condemning of others and their belief systems with which I disagree. I tolerate our differences, and assume that these people are as devoted to their worldviews as I am to mine. Sometimes I am even envious of the total engagement I see in some pilgrims. I enjoy reading about McGowan's dedication to her annual walk on the Chartres labyrinth, yet I am doubtful of the story she tells of its history.

I notice that if I stay in this disconnected state too long I get lonely. So then I am aware that I am experiencing more of a Procedural Connected Knowing. I think of ways to see the world from other people's perspective. In this state I want to be part of something bigger than myself. I long to be filled with that spiritual serenity that others seem to know and love. I want to have a mystical experience like McGowan has as she walks the labyrinth, dreaming of being a descendent of Mary Magdalene!

After I return home from the tour of French Cathedrals and their stained glass windows, I make plans to get back to that country and explore more of the sacred places affiliated with Mary Magdalene, according to McGowan, Brown and the medieval legends. I was feeling pulled back to France for my own pilgrimage.

I read extensively about the legends and feel captivated by the idea of going to southern France to see where she apparently did her ministry after Jesus died. I wanted to walk where she had walked and see where she served as an Apostle telling people of the good news of the resurrection of Jesus. I learn about the medieval Cathars who were very innocent people, inspired by Mary Magdalene's goodness, but slaughtered by the Roman Catholic Crusaders when they did not honor the Pope. I am intrigued to discover that there are tours to the mountaintops to see the ruined Cathar castles.[47]

I buy travel guides, novels, plays and books about the legends of her amazing ministry and people who followed her for centuries. I learn the various legends about the connection between Jerusalem and France. There are claims that after Jesus died on the cross that Jerusalem was a dangerous place for believers, so Mary Magdalene supposedly climbed in a boat and sailed away across the sea. There are variations to this story, but the most striking one is that she was in this boat with no rudder and she sailed across the Mediterranean Sea and landed in southern France. Then the legends tell us that she lived in a grotto (cave), flew up daily to the spiritual world, and returned to earth each evening to preach. She even preached to the Emperor Tiberius of Rome, with a red egg in her hand, and almost convinced him of Jesus' resurrection. My mind is overflowing with these legends![48]

I want to get back to France! I yearn to go on a journey completely focused on Mary Magdalene and these legends. In my awareness of my Connected Knowing, I think that I need this experience for capturing some of the intensity I felt when I walked the labyrinth. Maybe if I could see these southern French chapels, towers, grottos and relics, I would empathize with all the other devoted pilgrims who try to get close to Mary Magdalene. There is a mystery pulling me towards southern France.

I explore the internet and find that I could join a tour group led by a New-Age mystic claiming to be an expert on Mary Magdalene. I write a grant and am funded to go on this magical trip! We will visit all the sites and find our "inner Mary Magdalene" in a ritual performed on her special day, July 22nd. I am so excited! But then the more I read about these legends, and plan my trip, the more I sense my nagging doubts about the validity of these claims. How did these people actually know that she ever came to France? I have seen an alleged relic already and was not convinced. So why am I getting swept up in this wild fantasy?

Time out. Pay attention to my more logical side: Procedural Separate Knowing. What was I doing spending all this grant money going to a place that was so questionable in terms of really being relevant to the true Mary Magdalene? What was the evidence that she had ever lived in France? Even if the stories were nearly a thousand years old, does that make them true? Should I cancel my trip to France?

THEOLOGICAL TOOL

Currently, there are many historians who focus on the early Christian Church. One of them is Dr. Bart Ehrman who has published several books about Jesus and Mary Magdalene. He tells those of us who are not expert historians how we can try to sort through claims of past events in early Christian history. In simple terms, he suggests the following procedure for critically analyzing what we hear. These four questions help us to logically and systematically peel away the fiction from the more probable facts. 1) The older the documents and the evidence are, the better. 2) Evidence confirmed by several independent sources is more convincing. 3) Stories that "cut against the grain" and are contrary to what is completely predictable are more noteworthy. 4) Context is everything, as any newly discovered evidence needs to be considered in the context of what experts already agree is true about that particular point in history.[49]

Ehrman's guidelines for examining historical claims help me come to my senses and avoid being carried into this magical mystery tour of France. Using this logical, historical methods procedure of sorting through what I was reading about Mary Magdalene living and preaching in southern France, I become full of doubt. Although the legends were nearly a thousand years old and more than one independent source told the tales, I wonder how these storytellers knew what they knew? I dig deeper and can find absolutely nothing that fits in the context of information we learn from the canonical Gospels. Therefore, the legends may have met some aspects of Ehrman's criteria for confirming historical evidence but they did not meet the fourth one.

I make my decision. I contact the directors of the foundation providing funds for my journey and tell them that I am changing my mind about my trip to study Mary Magdalene. I do not need to use their funds to go to southern France ... I need to go to Israel! (More about that trip later!)

I am setting aside my books about the French legends. Lately, I am treating them as literary fantasies that are fun to read, but not adding to my deeper understanding of the essential Mary Magdalene. Although there are plenty of legends, I no longer think there is any true indication that she ever went to France or Rome. I do believe she inspired people in her ministry, but I am not certain where she did this.

I really appreciate this renewed awareness of my Procedural understanding acquired through both Separate and Connected Knowing because it helps me decide about my pilgrimage travels. Now I want to apply this heightened awareness of my two kinds of Procedural understanding to my research into doctrines — another type of journey.

PSYCHOLOGICAL TOOL

Dr. James Fowler (the developmental psychologist) explains his theory of the six stages of faith. In previous chapters, I summarized the first four stages:

1) Intuitive-Projective Faith
2) Mythic-Literal Faith
3) Synthetic-Conventional Faith
4) Individuative-Reflective Faith

Fowler asserts that people usually do not reach the fifth stage until midlife, if at all! He calls this Conjunctive Faith because there is conjunction or a re-integration of aspects of the fragmented self. Usually this involves a new fascination with powerful symbols, legends and rituals that are embraced as a means of expressing a more mature faith. It is not a regression back to a child-like belief, but a new combination of external and internal spiritual practices.[50]

 During my journey to France, when I wondered about the worship of Mary Magdalene's relics and I walked on the labyrinth, I felt a powerful longing to experience meaningful rituals. According to Fowler, this means that I was experiencing the stage of Conjunctive Faith. With this hunger for meaningful rituals and symbols, I was also more susceptible to a belief in the symbols described in *The Da Vinci Code*[51], such as the rose, the "V" shaped images, and the Holy Grail. The French medieval legends also refer to symbols of Mary Magdalene including the Tower of Magdala, a grotto, an alabaster jar of ointments, essential oils, a book, long red hair, a skull and a red egg. But I have since set aside those symbols that are part of literary fantasy from details in the stories in the canonical-Gospels that have deeper meaning for my spiritual life. I recognize that symbols can hold great meaning if we understand them, but I am not convinced that these are the right ones on which to focus. The next part of my journey involves searching for more important correspondences of the Easter story.[52]

PHILOSOPHICAL TOOL
Dr. Harry Moody (philosopher) offers his theory of the *Five Stages of the Soul*. After interviewing hundreds of elderly people, he describes five typical stages of spiritual growth. In earlier chapters I emphasized the first three stages that he labels: 1) "The Call," 2) "The Search" and 3) "The Struggle." In the fourth stage, people often experience "The Breakthrough." He says: "A Breakthrough is any experience of heightened awareness and sudden insight that fundamentally changes the way people look at themselves and the world around them."[53]

If Fowler and Moody are right, they would say I was experiencing both a time of "Conjunctive Faith" and a "Breakthrough". I appreciate these descriptions because I feel as if someone really understands me. These philosophers and psychologists give me a language beyond vague, over-used words like "Amazing" and "Awesome" to describe my recent journey of learning about my faith. Their theories help me elaborate on my search for the essential story of Mary Magdalene, whom I believe was the most devoted follower of the Lord God Jesus Christ.

I had a Breakthrough in my deeper understanding of rituals and symbols. This prepared me to look more closely at the canonical-Gospels in the *Holy Bible*, and search for their inner meanings. I was looking for true symbols and their correspondences.

THEOLOGICAL TOOL

Emanuel Swedenborg (theologian of the 18th century) emphasizes the internal sense of the *Holy Bible*. He claims that people can learn the literal stories and stop there, but these stories are like vessels holding sacred meanings. We can understand and then apply these meanings to our spiritual growth. For example, in Matthew 25: 35- 46, there is a description of Jesus telling people that we should feed the hungry, give water to the thirsty and welcome the stranger. Jesus explains that when we do these actions to other people we are symbolically doing it to Him. There is the literal story of charitably feeding and clothing our neighbors, but this story also holds a deeper meaning about our spiritual lives.[54]

Therefore, we are doing the Lord's will when we offer love (represented by food) and truth (represented by water) to other people and include them in our spiritual communities (represented by welcoming a stranger). I see that this could mean that a spiritual journey is not just a private introspection. It also involves how we treat other peo-ple.[55] I had studied Swedenborg's descriptions of correspon-dences before but I had never thought about examining Mary Magdalene using this theological source of Swedenborg's Writings. This was a Breakthrough for me! I can remember the day when this hit me. I immediately go and search for Swedenborgian references to Mary Magdalene.[56] It was quite a discovery. First of all, allow me to emphasize what was NOT included in this Swedenborgian reference material about the *Holy Bible.*

1) There was nothing about her sex life as an adulterer or prostitute.
2) There was nothing about her using the ointment from the alabaster jar.
3) There was nothing about her being married to Jesus or being pregnant.
4) There was nothing about her traveling to France to spread the good news.
5) There was nothing about her being a saint.
6) There was nothing about her representing a divine fem-inine spirit.
7) There was nothing about her holding a red egg when preaching.
8) There was nothing about a rose or "V" shape represent-ing her.
9) There was nothing about spiritual practices involving her relics.
10) There is no mention of her in relationship to the Holy Grail.

So this confirms my earlier search process in which I was peeling away the unsubstantiated legends, myths, symbols and novels. Now I am eager and ready, in my Breakthrough, to find out what is included in these Writings of Swedenborg. I am even more excited to understand Mary Magdalene's role with Jesus, and what it might mean for my spiritual growth. I know what she literally experienced in her interactions with

Him, but what was the spiritual correspondence? Where was this journey leading me?

As I read Swedenborg's writings, I discover four major details of her story and what they represent for us in our own spiritual growth. I will examine each point in the next chapters of this book. This is a new perspective that I have not seen published in any of the other books on my shelf about Mary Magdalene and I think it is worth our close inspection.

MARY MAGDALENE AT THE CROSS
JERUSALEM, ISRAEL

CHAPTER 4

Mary Magdalene Was
Spiritually Aware

On the morning of the summer solstice, my husband meets me in Paris. Neil has been on a business trip in Germany while I was on that group tour exploring the medieval cathedrals of France. But the highlight of that group trip was Paris and we are given a few glorious days to just explore the city on our own. If that wasn't enough of a promise of joy, my husband comes to join me. We had never been to Paris together before and it was wonderful, especially because it was also our wedding anniversary that week. I was ready for a memorable day.

Of course there is too much to see in Paris in a short time, so we start by going to the Cafe Palais Royal. We sip our strong coffee, explore our guidebooks and watch the people walk by, while sitting outside under an awning just a block from the Louvre. Most people already know that this museum is featured in Brown's mystery novel, *The DaVinci Code*. While most of the crowds were aiming for tours of the "V" shaped designs in the Louvre, we decide to go in another direction. We know that there is the possibility of visiting the

NEIL IN PARIS, FRANCE

Cathedral of Notre Dame, but I was just not very interested in churches dedicated to the Virgin Mary.

While casually flipping through the guidebook and wondering about our options, I see that there is a site called "L'Eglise de la St. Madeleine". Could there be any other Madeleine, or was this actually referring to Mary Magdalene? On the map, I could see that it was just a few blocks away, so we finish our refreshments and head out through the busy streets of Paris.

L'Eglise de la St. Madeleine, Paris, France

Pediment, L'Eglise de la St. Madeleine, Paris, France

L'Eglise de la St. Madeleine, painting by Werner
Paris, France

This neo-classical building looks exactly like a Roman Temple, with columns and a triangular pediment on which it says: "D.O.M.SVB.INVOC.S.N.MAGDALENAE".

A French friend tells me that this abbreviated message might mean: "A Dieu tout puissant sous l'invocation Saint Mary Magdalene" which translates as "A God so powerful under the invocation of Saint Mary Magdalene".

Inside there are no stained glass windows; in fact there are very few windows at all as it is not a Gothic style cathedral. We have to adjust our eyes, because it is very dark inside except for the spotlights focusing on an imposing statue at the other end of the huge room.

We see that it is a statue of Mary Magdalene being carried up to heaven by angels. This is a visual image of the legend that is widely believed across this country. Many accept the story that she traveled to France after the resurrection, and lived in a grotto. They claim that she prayed daily, and during her meditations she was carried up to the heavens. Although the statue is stunning to look at, I still do not agree with this legend and am feeling disheartened that this is the focal point of the enormous building dedicated to her. Why have they chosen this legend to demonstrate in their artwork, when they had the entire Easter story that is so much more compelling?

Neil and I want to know more about the history of this Roman style building that feels so out of place in this part of Paris. Apparently, about 200 years ago, Napoleon had it built as a monument for the glory of the army. He wanted viewers to be impressed by how it looked like the ancient Roman structures built when that empire dominated much of the western world. It was a political building constructed around the same time as the much more famous Arche de Triomphe. But after the fall of Napoleon's empirical leadership, the church claimed it. Then with the official pronouncement from King Louis XVIII, it became the Church of Saint Mary Magdalene, or L'Eglise de la St. Madeleine, around 1847. So it has been dedicated to her for just over 150 years. By European standards, this is a relatively short time period for an historical building and apparently it has not changed much during that era.[57]

MARY MAGDALENE BEING CARRIED BY ANGELS, PAINTING BY WERNER
L'EGLISE DE LA ST. MADELEINE, PARIS, FRANCE

MARY MAGDALENE BEING CARRIED BY ANGELS
TROYES, FRANCE

ently, L'Eglise de la St. Madeleine still functions as a ...ch on rare occasions, as some of the more fashionable Parisians use it as a setting for weddings. But with Catholic Church attendance down to about 10% of their French members, there are not many church services there these days. There are no devoted worshippers present when we walk through the church. I hear that the vast majority of urban French people seem to be somewhat indifferent to theological study and worship. So now this church is more like a secular museum with a restaurant in the lower level, and a focus on the tale of Mary Magdalene flying up to heaven from a French grotto.

Then it struck me. That may be why they chose this image for their most featured statue in L'Eglise de la St. Madeleine. I am already aware of the intense pride people hold for their French culture and history, and these stories of Mary Magdalene arriving in southern France must have become even more important to them than the stories of her witnessing the Lord's resurrection in Israel. It was a conscious emphasis on the French leaders' part to glorify the history of France, even if these were just legends. The French leaders and artists were using her name to bring attention and political honor to their own culture's legendary history. I appreciate their national pride, but I feel they missed the mark. I think that in their enthusiasm for glorifying France, they misdirected the focus of their spotlight away from the more important story of Mary Magdalene.

Ψ PSYCHOLOGICAL TOOL

Around half a century ago, Dr. Benjamin Bloom and a group of other educational psychologists described taxonomies that outline hierarchies of the affective and cognitive dimensions of human knowledge. They concluded that there are five levels of complexity or intensity in the "Affective Domain". People increasingly engage their emotions when they learn about the world and then react to it. Read from the bottom up on this step-like hierarchy of human emotions in the Affective Domain:

5) Highest level: CHARACTERIZING
4) Next level: ORGANIZING VALUES
3) Next level: VALUING
2) Next level: RESPONDING
1) Lowest level: RECEIVING

When a person is at the lowest levels of emotional engagement, she is "Receiving", which means observing, attending, listening and being alert. At the next level, she is "Responding", which involves being even more willing to obey and comply with what is taught, and more deeply considering issues with full awareness. At the third level, she may choose to "Value" what is presented to her by others, by being devoted and accepting with a full heart. At the highest and most sophisticated levels, a person is "Organizing" her life around her chosen values, and then "Characterizing" herself as a devoted follower of a chosen belief system.[58]

 While Neil and I are investigating L'Eglise de la St. Madeleine, we are both very curious about this building: its history, the architecture, the statue inside, the pediment above the entrance, and the building's relationship to its patron saint—Mary Magdalene. Bloom would say that we are functioning at the first two levels of the "Affective Domain Taxonomy": Receiving and Responding. We know we have hundreds of places we can see in Paris, but we purposely go to this sacred site and are ready with enthusiasm to learn and "Receive". Then after we soak up all we can, we "Respond" with our affections. We are feeling intrigued, engaged and willing to learn about why this building was featured in the middle of Paris. But, in terms of my own affectional response, I must admit that I was feeling disappointment. I just cannot go to the next level on Bloom's taxonomy because I do not have the same experience of "Valuing" this building as much as the French citizens do. The statue of the legendary history of Mary Magdalene in a southern French grotto was just not as important to me as the Easter story in the canonical

Gospels. So we leave L'Eglise de la St. Madeleine with a sigh.

What did I wish had been featured in that church in Paris? After I sort through all the legends, the novels, and the confusing statements from Roman Catholic Popes and clergy, what am I left with? The essential Easter story.

 It occurs to me that I can also apply Bloom's Taxonomy of the Affective Domain to my analysis of Mary Magdalene's emotions. The authors of all four of the canonical Gospels imply that she was spiritually "Receiving" (using Bloom's term). She was ready to Receive as she was serving as a witness. She was present during his crucifixion, and was intently focusing her attention on His burial. After the Sabbath on Saturday, she got up early on Sunday morning, even before dawn's early light, and went to see His body and possibly anoint it. Some historians have guessed that sundown of the Sabbath prevented her from anointing him immediately, so she had to wait for Sunday morning, according to Jewish customs. Apparently she missed Him terribly and was grieving for the loss of her teacher.

MARY MAGDALENE AT THE CROSS
PAINTING BY WERNER

MARY MAGDALENE IS WORRIED ABOUT WHERE JESUS HAS GONE
PAINTING BY WERNER

 What did she Receive through her senses when she approached the sepulcher? According to the statements in the canonical Gospels of the *Holy Bible*, she Received the sensation of a violent earthquake (Matthew 28). In addition, she Received the sensation of seeing one or more bright angels at the entrance of the sepulcher. The angels were in shiny white garments, according to all four of the canonical Gospels:

. . . for an angel of the Lord came down from heaven and, going to the tomb, rolled back the stone and sat on it. His appearance was like lightning, and his clothes were white as snow. (*Holy Bible*, Matthew 28)

. . . they saw a young man dressed in a white robe . . . (*Holy Bible*, Mark 16)

. . . two men in clothes that gleamed like lightning stood beside them. (*Holy Bible*, Luke 24)

. . . saw two angels in white . . . (*Holy Bible*, John 20)

The angels talked to her, saying:

"Woman, why are you crying?" (*Holy Bible*, John 20).

"Do not be afraid, for I know that you are looking for Jesus, who was crucified. He is not here; He has risen, just as He said. Come and see the place where He lay." (*Holy Bible*, Matthew 28)

"Don't be alarmed . . . You are looking for Jesus the Nazarene, who was crucified. He has risen! He is not here. See the place where they laid him." (*Holy Bible*, Mark 16)

"Why do you look for the living among the dead? He is not here; he has risen!" (*Holy Bible*, Luke 24)[59]

Mary Magdalene felt this violent earthquake, saw brightly clothed angels, and heard them explain that she would not find His body here. He had risen from the dead! Certainly the literal story itself is remarkable enough, but what do these events that she witnessed and Received symbolize at a spiritual level? Is there an internal sense? Are we worthy of understanding it as she did?

THEOLOGICAL TOOL

Emanuel Swedenborg, the theologian from the 1700's, provides an interpretation of this story. He tells us that the literal story is certainly miraculous but it has an internal, spiritual meaning for us all. If we are eagerly receptive to the meaning of the symbols in the *Holy Bible,* we can learn, respond and apply them to our lives. As a result we can grow spiritually, if we choose. Swedenborg teaches us that the shiny white garments that clothed the angels at the sepulcher correspond to genuine truth. If Mary Magdalene saw the illuminated garments with her spiritual eyes opened, then she was certainly in a receptive state to begin to understand deeper truths. And as she witnessed the earthquake, this corresponds to her having her spiritual senses opened enough so that she could understand that the state of the church was about to change dramatically. It was like an announcement of things to come.[60]

MARY MAGDALENE IS AFRAID DURING THE EARTHQUAKE
PAINTING BY WERNER

MARY MAGDALENE IS SURPRISED WHEN SHE MEETS AN ANGEL
PAINTING BY WERNER

In earlier chapters I explained how several psychologists and philosophers offer developmental theories to help us understand people more thoroughly. Let's apply some of them along with Swedenborg's ideas to further our understanding of Mary Magdalene's experiences that Easter morning.

From the philosopher Moody's perspective, Mary Magdalene was experiencing the first stages: The Call, the Search and the Struggle. The "Call" and the "Search" refer to the time when she went to the sepulcher to find Jesus' body. She was seeking his body and missing the way He would teach her. Her spiritual eyes were opened to whatever she would find that morning. When she was conversing with the angels she may have been "Struggling" to understand where His body has been laid, and what was happening; this is similar to Moody's third stage of faith.[61]

Mary Magdalene was apparently experiencing at least three of Moody's stages of faith in that one morning, when she felt the earthquake and talked to the angels in very bright garments. It must have been both terrifying and joyful to see the earthquake and these brilliant spirits. If her spiritual eyes were opened she could more completely comprehend what this all meant. Apparently she was being invited by the Lord Jesus Christ to see genuine truth and to bear witness that now it was time for an enormous change to happen in the state of the church on earth. This was like a proclamation and she was the first human being to ever Receive it!

Mary Belenky is the psychologist who described many ways that women know what they know. I can also apply her theory to this description of Mary Magdalene's experiences at the sepulcher. I am picturing this scene of Mary Magdalene rushing there as a woman who was at first focusing on her "Received Knowledge". Jesus had taught her for years during His ministry along the Sea of Galilee. We have no quotes from Mary Magdalene speaking in the canonical Gospels of the *Holy Bible* until she is talking to the angels near the sepulcher. So we don't exactly know how she was reacting to all that she had Received from Jesus, because we have no earlier dialog.

However, Mary's commitment to Jesus led her to follow Him even through the crucifixion, burial and resurrection.[62]

I also like to apply Belenky's psychological theory to explain that when Mary Magdalene's spiritual eyes were opened and she saw the earthquake and the brightly clothed angels, that this might also have been like an "Inner Voice" illuminating her mind and presenting the spiritual correspondences. I think that she was experiencing an enlightened state, which is a very rare privilege. This may have felt like what Belenky calls "Subjective Knowledge: Inner Voice". Swedenborg tells us that Mary Magdalene saw bright garments as white as snow, and this meant that she was absorbing genuine truths into her mind. I read this to mean that she was trusted to experience this inner enlightenment of truth, because Jesus could read her thoughts and decided that she was so sincere that she would not falsify what she was Receiving.

I think that this is actually the danger of most "Subjective Knowledge": just because something occurs to us in our inner thoughts and imagination does not always mean that it is true. But Swedenborg reassures us with his interpretation of the *Holy Bible* that Mary Magdalene was sincere, and spiritually Receptive to genuine truths and she understood their correspondence. She could interpret the earthquake as a symbol that the state of the church was about to change, greatly.

Bloom and the educational psychologists who outlined the "Affective Domain Taxonomy" might concur with Belenky but use their own terminology to explain the remarkable events at the sepulcher. I think they would say that Mary Magdalene was not only Receiving ideas from His ministry, but she also showed a definite indication of emotionally "Responding" and "Valuing" what she Received. This prompted Mary Magdalene to rush to the sepulcher and look for Him. I would even assert that she was experiencing the highest levels on the "Affective Domain Taxonomy", because she seemed to be "Organizing" and "Characterizing" her life around the values and doctrines she learned from Jesus Christ. In general, she seems to be the first human being to believe that He was actually rising from the dead and would prepare a place for us all in the afterlife. She seems absolutely confident that He was the promised Messiah and went to tell the disciples!

Swedenborg tells us that Mary Magdalene was given this privilege because she was so devoted and sincere. She was granted the chance to have her spiritual eyes opened because Jesus trusted her to be careful with these genuine truths and not destroy them in some selfish way. I conclude that He chose her because she was worthy.

PSYCHOLOGICAL TOOL

In the 1950's to the 1970's, at Harvard University, developmental psychologists began to do research and then outline stages of typical moral development. They were approaching this endeavor from a completely secular point of view, using examples of how people think, feel and act in their moral dilemmas with other people. Dr. Lawrence Kohlberg was a confirmed atheist but he noticed how boys and men seemed to go through six stages as they matured in their moral orientations. In the sixth stage, the men seem to "Seek Universal Truth and Justice". Although Kohlberg himself was not seeking truth, he had to respect the fact that this search for universal truth was apparently important to the most morally mature people he interviewed. One of his graduate students followed in this line of research but focused on a more feminine form of moral maturation. Dr. Carol Gilligan interviewed girls and women and noticed that the most morally mature people make critical decisions based on their value of intense "CARE" for their relationships with others. Since these psychologists published their theories decades ago, other psychologists have critiqued them and continued to study these gender distinctions in moral development. Many positive psychologists feel that morally and spiritually mature men and women need to do both: "Seek Universal Truths" and "Care" about people.[63]

Even though many of these modern day psychologists are not overtly religious, we can use their tools as we apply their theories of moral development, feminine forms of thinking and caring, and affective learning to a person's spiritual growth. As I apply them in my analysis of Mary Magdalene's life, it enriches my appreciation of her experiences. Clearly in this part of the Easter story, she is devotedly searching for Jesus' body to care for it with ointments. She is ready to Receive anything she can find out, but she serendipitously discovers powerful truths through her spiritual vision. Kohlberg and Gilligan might describe her experience in terms of her "Seeking Universal Truths" and "Caring" for Jesus, whom she loved. However, I do not feel satisfied that they completely capture all the layers of her experience. Therefore, I turn to the Biblical interpretations offered by Swedenborg to enrich my comprehension of her role.

I realize that I am not the only one who is searching for this level of depth in a theological quest, so I take time to join other seekers.

During a summer holiday a few years back, I decided to go on a spiritual retreat with 50 other women who are readers of Swedenborg's Writings. We meet in a rural setting called "Purley Chase House", north of Oxford, England. In this comfortable setting we talk, share and worship together. We are all familiar with Swedenborg's work but vary in terms of which books we study, whether we think they are divine revelation, and how we apply the ideas. There is an intense feeling of belonging in this group of female seekers, even with our variations in approaches to the Writings. Some women are more intent on rediscovering meaningful rituals such as sacred dance, while other women want to derive doctrines to help them with their current life challenges. Still other seekers on the retreat are historians and love to see the influence that Swedenborg's writings have on well-known people such as Ralph Waldo Emerson and

Dietrich Bonhoeffer. I love this retreat and wish it would last all summer long. I feel enriched with my sense of spiritual belonging even if I never get to see all of these wonderful women again. I tell some of the women about my search for Mary Magdalene and they listen with keen interest.

PSYCHOLOGICAL TOOL
During the 1950's, Dr. Abraham Maslow was one of the first humanistic psychologists to offer a theory describing our human needs in a hierarchy of importance and urgency. He claims that people must address their lower needs before paying attention to their higher needs. Read this model about human needs from the bottom up, on this hierarchy:

5) Highest level: SELF ACTUALIZATION
4) Next higher level: NEED FOR SELF-ESTEEM
3) Next higher level: NEED TO BELONG
2) Next higher level: SAFETY NEEDS
1) Lowest level: PHYSIOLOGICAL NEEDS

Maslow was asserting that once a person's basic needs for safety and physiological drives are addressed and not a distraction, that there is a compelling need for a sense of belonging to a group, a need to acquire self esteem, and finally there is a yearning to actualize oneself while fulfilling one's potential. This striving for the higher needs on the hierarchy can be visited periodically, but actually take a lifetime to achieve.[64]

I am so content on this retreat in England because I feel like I am satisfying my need to "Belong" with other women who were spiritual seekers. Many of us have read Swedenborg's Writings and find them to be useful tools for the questions that are puzzling us. We honor each other's individual quests and offer mutual support as we share what we are each learning. No one tries to overpower us or take away our spiritual freedom, which I deeply appreciate.

Each of us feels esteemed by the other seekers present, and it is assumed we are all striving to live up to our spiritual potential, especially as women. Maslow would most likely say that we are all working, side by side, on addressing our needs to "Belong", to achieve "Self Esteem", and maybe to try to "Self Actualize".

However, Maslow was like many psychologists of the twentieth century as he usually shied away from discussing people's spiritual growth. So I appreciate his description of what I am experiencing at a social and personal level but it does not quite cover it all. I am also addressing my needs at a spiritual level in my longing to understand and serve the Lord more effectively. After hearing others speak, I tell a few of my fellow retreat members what I am learning about Mary Magdalene and I feel their warm empathy for my search to understand this compelling role model in my life.

 Using Maslow's terms in analyzing Mary Magdalene's life, Mary Magdalene "Belonged" to a group of people who followed Jesus near the Sea of Galilee, so she probably did not feel alone. Yet she was spiritually evolving in a way not adequately described by Maslow. First she was possessed by seven demons, and then Jesus cast them out. Later she heard his sermons and longed to hear more as she developed her faith. She was increasingly humble and receptive to His teachings. Jesus must have seen this quality in her and blessed her with the opportunity to see even more potent genuine truths, and to interpret this as the impending change of state in the church. She was not striving for "Esteem" in terms of promoting herself, but she was "Actualizing" her potential by freely choosing to understand His teachings.

Swedenborg tells us that intelligence and wisdom are actually all from the Divine. We can perceive truth, learn to love it, and then live according to what we understand to be true. What we know becomes wisdom when we acknowledge the source of all truth as Divine, and apply it to our lives, without taking credit by thinking of ourselves as brilliant.[65] Our esteem then lies in our value as living receptacles of truth and goodness that come from the Divine. We can have esteem and grateful humility at the same time.

 For the climactic experience on this spiritual retreat in rural England, a dozen women dress up on Sunday morning and dramatically portray key Biblical women who interacted with Jesus Christ. One of them acts out a convincing Mary Magdalene and I am moved to tears watching the drama. I am so delighted with this theatrical interpretation because of the selection of focusing on Mary Magdalene in the Easter story. The actress/seeker on this retreat does not choose to illustrate any of the tales of Mary Magdalene from French legends, the modern historical fiction novels, the Gnostic documents, the secret societies, or the Roman Catholic mistaken sermons. This wonderful seeker narrates what I think of as the most important elements of the story involving Mary Magdalene:

* Coming to the tomb.
* Spiritually seeing brightly clothed angels.
* Talking to the angels and Jesus.
* Witnessing the earthquake.

My fellow seeker acts out my favorite story using the sources of the canonical Gospels of the *Holy Bible* and Swedenborg's Writings that interpret the *Holy Bible*. She confirms for me how important it is to have a positive, female role model, especially one that I can picture clearly. Later in the day, I thank the woman who acted out Mary Magdalene in her dramatic narration.

Upon reflection, I conclude that Mary Magdalene was reaching her potential and thus she was self-actualizing ... by Receiving genuine truths that came directly from the Lord Jesus Christ. She was spiritually aware.

CHAPTER 5

Mary Magdalene Was
Spiritually Accepting

Our spiritual retreat for 50 female seekers in rural England is coming to an end all too soon. I attempt to get grounded back into reality after some heavenly experiences. I pack my bags and we exit in our rental car across the countryside. I am traveling with a few other middle-aged women and we are planning to spend the night in my cousin's little cottage near Oxford. I feel so reluctant to have to think about the annoying details of luggage, ground transportation, and sitting in a small seat on the long plane ride back to the USA in a day or so. I try to stay cheerful, but I long to be back at that serene retreat meditating on Mary Magdalene.

After my brief visit to my cousin's cottage, the next day her husband kindly offers to take me to the bus depot in Oxford so I can ride from there to the London airport. As we drive into the city where he is employed at Oxford University Press, he points out the famous sites. In his thick British accent he says, "On our left is the Maudlin College of Oxford University. There is a famous tower at the chapel there but it is not always open to visitors." I can see it from a distance and it appears like a typical Gothic cathedral. I am not too interested at the time and worrying more about the bus schedule and whether I have enough British currency. We just

MAGDALEN TOWER
PAINTING BY WERNER
OXFORD, ENGLAND

whiz by the tower and it is all a blur.

When I return back home to America, I investigate what we had driven by so quickly. I wonder: What was "Maudlin" anyway? So I look in my reference books and on the internet. I discover that this is a variation on the pronunciation of Mary Magdalene's name! Both Oxford and Cambridge have colleges named after her, and they spell it Magdalen College but pronounce it "Maudlin". I dig deeper and find out that around 1448 there was a place called Magdalen Hall, which eventually became Magdalen College a decade later. Due to political turmoil the rest of the buildings were not constructed until 1467. Almost a hundred years later, the Anglican Church pulled away from the Roman Catholic Church under King Henry VIII. Some time after that, this chapel at the Magdalen College became affiliated with the Anglican Church. They installed some linenfold panelings and Renaissance carvings, and five of them illustrate the life of Mary Magdalene. I wish I had seen them![66]

The only photograph of any artwork at this college that I can find on the internet is a weathered sculpture of her holding a jar of ointment. It is in a stone archway above a gateway into St. John's Quad at Magdalen College. I feel a bit of relief. In contrast to the way that the French people focus on a legend in their Church of Mary Magdalene to promote their nation's history, at least the British people were not promoting their own history when they named their college after her 1500 years ago. Her name was well known in theological circles, so they simply used it for one of their many colleges at Oxford.

By including a sculpture of her with a jar, at least we can observe it and think about her coming to anoint Jesus' body in the sepulcher. However, this image could still be confused with the unnamed female sinner who anointed His feet at a dinner party, and this conflation still disturbs me. Observers simply do not seem to make the distinction, but I feel it is important.

In British history, by the time many English had pulled away from the Roman Catholic Church and established the Anglican Church, they had the option of distancing themselves from Papal authority. They could have rejected the sermons of Pope Gregory from the 6th century, in which he declared that Mary Magdalene was an adulterer or prostitute. I am left wondering about this detail, and may never know.

But I do find it intriguing that the British people use the name of Magdalene at Oxford University even if there is not much information about who she was on the official website of this college. Instead the webmasters list all the famous Nobel Peace Prize winners who are alumni of Magdalen College. This place has become a world-renowned center of academic study, and yet the educational leaders do not seem to promote extensive study of her life and what it could mean to us today. This seems like a missed opportunity as they emphasize more secular studies and worldly accomplishments. Her name is very present, but there is no obvious mention of her as the chosen witness to the resurrection. I am not likely to make another trip to Oxford University. It actually feels like I probably did not miss much when I went driving by their famous chapel, at least in terms of my quest to understand more about the essential Mary Magdalene.[67] Maybe I will visit the Magdalen College of Cambridge University at some time in the future. I would like to see the stained glass windows there and study what stories they illustrate. Perhaps they are focused on the Easter story.

PSYCHOLOGICAL TOOL

Dr. James Fowler is the developmental psychologist who offers us his description of the six stages of faith. In earlier chapters I described the details of his first five stages. Fowler describes the sixth stage as "Universalizing Faith". He explains that there are very few people who evolve to this point. People who are in this stage seem liberated from any social, political and economic shackles of life. They look beyond this materialistic world and instead seek universal justice and love. They are no longer concerned with seeking honor, fame or material wealth. They want to see a transformation of this world, led and inspired by the Divine. "They embody the promise and lure of shared futurity . . . and they trust the power of the future".[68]

The canonical Gospels tell us that Mary Magdalene was the first human being to witness Jesus Christ while He was in the process of ascending to heaven. Jesus was demonstrating that there is an afterlife and that we can all believe in it. She had seen the earthquake and the brightly clothed angels, and realized that it meant there would be a change in the state of the church. Now she could comprehend the genuine truth that everyone could look forward to a future in the afterlife. According to Fowler, Mary Magdalene may have been in the sixth stage of "Universalizing" faith, as she trusted in the promise of the future of a life beyond the grave. This truth was revealed to her and she accepted it, spiritually.

In the canonical Gospel of John of the *Holy Bible*, we read:

> She turned around and saw Jesus standing there, but she did not realize that it was Jesus. He asked her, "Woman, why are you crying? Who is it you are looking for?" Thinking he was the gardener, she said, "Sir, if you have carried him away, tell me where you have put him, and I will get him." Jesus said to her, "Mary." She turned toward him and cried out in Aramaic, "Rabboni!" (which means "Teacher"). Jesus said, "Do not hold on to me, for I have not yet ascended to the Father." (*Holy Bible*, John 20:14-17)

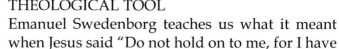THEOLOGICAL TOOL
Emanuel Swedenborg teaches us what it meant when Jesus said "Do not hold on to me, for I have not yet ascended to the Father." (*Holy Bible*: John 20: 17). People have debated for nearly 2000 years about whether Jesus was just a man or actually Divine. In this simple phrase He tells Mary Magdalene not to touch Him because he is still in the process of ascending. This means that Jesus is uniting His Human self with His Divine self. He is

explaining to her that his physical body must die in order to glorify His Human. He is urging her to shift her focus from this physical world to the spiritual world.[69]

 Mary Magdalene's spiritual eyes were opened so that she could receive genuine truth. After interacting with the angels in bright white clothing she was alert and ready. And then it came. Jesus was showing and telling her the most magnificent idea, that there is life after death. When He instructed her not to try to touch his ascending body, she was learning that we should not be so attached to the material, economic and political trappings of this world. The message is that there is a future and it is so much more meaningful than anything else on this earth. But people need to let go of the cares of this world, and that can be challenging.

PSYCHOLOGICAL TOOL
In the middle of the 20th century, Dr. Erik Erikson was a European psychologist who moved to America. He left behind his former colleague, Sigmund Freud and his pessimistic theories of psychoanalysis. Erikson spent his professional life analyzing the emotional issues presented to most people. Eventually he outlined the most complete theory of psychological development yet offered in the western world. Erikson describes eight stages of human life in terms of emotional struggles:
1) Infants: Trust vs. Mistrust
2) Toddlers: Autonomy vs. Shame
3) Preschoolers: Initiative vs. Guilt
4) Older Children: Competency vs. Inferiority
5) Adolescents: Identity vs. Role Confusion
6) Early Adults: Intimacy vs. Isolation
7) Adults: Generativity vs. Stagnation
8) Elders: Integrity vs. Despair
Erikson feels that in that final stage, an elderly person's struggle is about looking back on life and feeling despair

about a meaningless life, or integrity for living a life according to principles and values. However, Erikson does not mention elders looking into the future towards an afterlife.[70]

MARY MAGDALENE IS IN AWE AS SHE TRIES TO TOUCH THE GARMENTS OF JESUS
PAINTING BY WERNER

MARY MAGDALENE AS SHE TRIES TO TOUCH THE GARMENTS OF JESUS
MOSAIC IN FRANCE

MARY MAGDALENE AS SHE TRIES TO TOUCH THE GARMENTS OF JESUS
TROYES, FRANCE

MARY MAGDALENE MEETS AN ANGEL AND THEN MEETS JESUS IN THE GARDEN
FRANCE

 I am eager to apply Fowler's theory of the sixth stage of faith and Erikson's theory of the eighth stage of emotional development to help me comprehend Mary Magdalene's experience. When she is at that amazing moment of communicating with Jesus while He is rising from the grave, she seems to be letting go of any previous "Despair". In addition, she is observing a "transformation of the present reality in the direction of transcendent actuality".[71] Her spiritual eyes are opening and she understands this amazing truth: that Jesus is ascending and that we can join Him in the afterlife. He instructs her not to touch His garment, which means she should no longer consider Him just a man that walked the earth. The uniting of His Human self with his Divine Self was becoming a transcendent reality. She had the privilege of being the first witness to this glorification.

PHILOSOPHICAL TOOL
Dr. Harry Moody is the philosopher who offers his theory of the five *Stages of the Soul*. In previous chapters I described and applied his first three stages: "The Call", "The Search", and "The Struggle". His fourth stage is "The Breakthrough" and the fifth stage is "The Return". Moody claims that enlightenment and a new appreciation of God's Providence are key elements in "The Breakthrough" and "The Return".[72]

 While Mary Magdalene was the witness to this spiritual transformation during His ascension, she was also being spiritually transformed by what she learned. I believe it was like "The Breakthrough" described by Moody, which was made possible by her spiritual vision and comprehension of genuine truth.

This momentary event is so phenomenal in Mary Magdalene's life that in contrast all the legends, tales and mistaken identities falsely attributed to her just seem irrelevant to me. I keep wondering how we allow ourselves to be so distracted away from this essential story of transformation. Are we more fascinated with sex scandals, dramatic exits across the sea, rumors of a sacred union, and secret bloodlines?

It takes some discernment on our part to sort through all that we hear about Mary Magdalene, ignoring the fantasies, and then carefully selecting the most important story of all. I believe that the essential story is that she was invited to bear witness to His ascension and glorification, and she was permitted to comprehend that there is a future in the afterlife for us all. She was spiritually aware and spiritually accepting.

CHAPTER 6

Mary Magdalene Was Spiritually Acting

When I was on that group tour across France to see the medieval stained glass windows in 2008, I knew that I was supposed to be in the role of a follower. There were about 30 of us, and at least 3 leaders. I was in very capable hands. People took care of where I would sleep, eat and travel. I am not used to going to foreign countries on my own, since I only got my first passport when I was 40. I really appreciated Richard, Michael and Lisa as they told us where to go each day, and what to appreciate in the cathedrals.

But I remember the day when Richard was leading us on a walking tour of Troyes, France. I see beautiful buildings constructed about a thousand years ago. The village has little alleys and Tudor style architecture. I feel like I am walking into a fairy tale. Then the guide surprises me and takes us into a small Church that was dedicated to Mary Magdalene! We only have a few minutes as a group to explore it and I just cannot take pictures fast enough. So later that afternoon, when I have some unscheduled time, I

A STREET NAMED AFTER MARY MAGDALENE
TROYES, FRANCE

follow the map of Troyes and walk back to this lovely church. The garden outside is in full summer bloom. It is nearly empty in the chapel area but the signs say they welcome visitors. I have plenty of time to investigate.

I was giggling because I was feeling so brave to walk through this medieval town by myself. I do not speak French and was certain I would get lost. But I didn't, and it was so

GARDEN OUTSIDE CATHEDRAL OF MARY MAGDALENE
TROYES, FRANCE

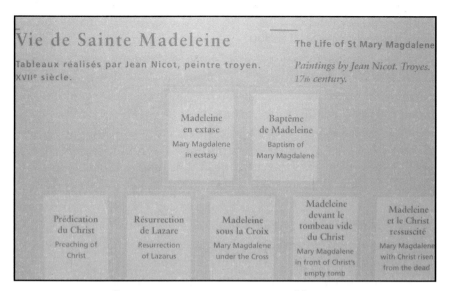

Vie de Sainte Madeleine — The Life of St Mary Magdalene

Tableaux réalisés par Jean Nicot, peintre troyen. XVIIᵉ siècle. — Paintings by Jean Nicot. Troyes. 17th century.

| Madeleine en extase / Mary Magdalene in ecstasy | Baptême de Madeleine / Baptism of Mary Magdalene |

| Prédication du Christ / Preaching of Christ | Résurrection de Lazare / Resurrection of Lazarus | Madeleine sous la Croix / Mary Magdalene under the Cross | Madeleine devant le tombeau vide du Christ / Mary Magdalene in front of Christ's empty tomb | Madeleine et le Christ ressuscité / Mary Magdalene with Christ risen from the dead |

SIGN EXPLAINING THE PAINTINGS OF NICOT
TROYES, FRANCE

exciting to venture out on my own for once. I adore this small Gothic style building and start to take pictures of the paintings and stained glass work depicting Mary Magdalene's life. I discover a series of paintings by Jean Nicot from the 17th century and some dazzling stained glass that was probably a thousand years old. (I have pictures of these paintings and stained glass incorporated throughout this book.) Although I do not agree with all of the images, there seem to be some unusual ones here that I have not seen anywhere else: Way up high I see a window illustrating a scene of Mary Magdalene telling people about the resurrection! I have never seen this part of the story in stained glass before. What a treasure!

Years later, I reflect on this solitary adventure. I usually depend on tour guides to lead me through foreign countries, but I could sense my courage increasing. I was beginning to think about going to other places on my own. I have wrestled with the idea of going to see the location of the legends in southern France, but once my goal was absolutely clear, I did decide to go to Israel. It took a long time to plan it, but I figured out how to do my own personal pilgrimage.

This is why, in spring of 2011, I go to the Middle East and

explore the Holy Land. It is exhilarating to be leading and planning all the details of this adventure by myself. After visiting the churches dedicated to Mary Magdalene in Paris and Troyes in 2008, I want to see any churches like this in Israel. I admit to hiring a local tour guide for the first couple of days in Israel, but eventually I am on my own.

I discover that there is a stunning cathedral built on the Mount of Olives in Jerusalem that I just have to see in person. This shrine dedicated to Mary Magdalene is only open to the public a couple of hours per week, so I plan my entire journey around that schedule. I have to arrive on Thursday morning or the nuns will not let me inside!

The Cathedral of Mary Magdalene is such a unique place. I am delighted to see that the Eastern/Russian Orthodox Church manages this nunnery and shrine. This is not the same branch of Christianity as the Roman Catholic Church, and therefore they do not acknowledge the authority of the Pope. I consider this to be an important point. It means that when this cathedral was constructed to honor her, the Russian people did not pay any attention to what Pope Gregory said in the 6th century about Mary Magdalene being a sinner! Therefore none of the artwork inside is illustrating that story. I do not see any images of a repentant adultress.

So how did this Russian style building get constructed in Israel? I learn that over a century ago the Romanoff royal family of Russia decided to build a monastery and cathedral on the Mount of Olives of Jerusalem. One of their female family members adored Mary Magdalene and wanted to have a place devoted to her so they could all visit it when they did their pilgrimages. The builders borrowed the architectural style of many Russian churches and built this cathedral with brilliant, gold, onion-shaped dome towers. Outside there is a lovely garden and home for nuns built on the steep hillside of the mountain. This sacred site is in the same location where Jesus, Mary Magdalene and the disciples may have rested and prayed among the olive trees. Over the entry to this shrine is a mosaic of Mary holding the alabaster jar, referring to her attempt to anoint His body in the sepulcher. Inside there is a

CATHEDRAL OF MARY MAGDALENE, SKETCH BY WERNER
JERUSALEM, ISRAEL

MARY MAGDALENE, PEDIMENT OF CATHEDRAL OF MARY MAGDALENE
JERUSALEM, ISRAEL

collection of large paintings high up on the walls illustrating scenes of Jesus and Mary Magdalene. I do not see any electric lights, but the sunshine pours through a few clearstory windows. I am partially blinded by this intense sunbeam while I examine the paintings.[73]

By this time on my pilgrimage I am getting used to immediately sorting through scenes I see illustrated in artwork in various buildings. I am pleased to see a painting of Jesus appearing to Mary Magdalene as He told her not to touch Him while He was still ascending. This is the story I was hoping they would feature so visitors could have this in their minds when they come to learn about her. I feel deep gratitude for the Eastern/Russian Orthodox Church for making this choice. Although it is challenging to photograph this painting way up high near sunny windows, it is still a thrill to see one of my favorite scenes featured in the Cathedral of Mary Magdalene.

 However, I do not agree with everything illustrated here. I also see a large painting of the legend of Mary Magdalene visiting Rome to preach to the Emperor Tiberius. The story goes that she came to tell the Emperor about the resurrection of Jesus and how His body was not found at the sepulcher but had risen. She held an egg in her hand as a symbol of rebirth and resurrection. The Emperor laughed and said, "That miracle is as likely to have happened as that egg is to turn bright red." And then it did! Everyone was shocked.[74]

Apparently this legend of her visiting Rome eventually led to our current practice of coloring Easter eggs! I never knew this connection before. Although I have enjoyed dying eggs with my daughters every year, I have to admit that I am skeptical about this ancient legend. But I do appreciate the nerve she must have had to go preach to anyone, much less the Emperor of Rome, knowing that people might scoff at her. Now that's courage. I have no evidence that she went before Emperor Tiberius, but I do like to think of her as brave.

I do feel immense gratitude for how this gorgeous cathedral stands out across all of Jerusalem and mostly draws attention to the role of Mary Magdalene in the Easter story. I also really appreciate how the Russian royal family and nuns have carefully featured a painting of Mary Magdalene meeting the risen Jesus, and they have NOT included anything about the confusion of her as the sinning women in the *Holy Bible*. I just wish they had left out the painting of the legend of her going to Rome.

PHILOSOPHICAL TOOL

Dr. Harry Moody gave us his description of the *Five Stages of the Soul*. In earlier chapters I explained the first four stages that Moody named: "The Call", "The Search", "The Struggle" and "The Breakthrough". He describes the final stage as "The Return", which is a phase when a person can choose whether to share her spiritual awakenings with others. After coming close to the Divine and experiencing tremendous insights,

"The Return" involves going back to one's own community or family, and then addressing earthly problems with great insights. Moody uses the example of the character Ebeneezer Scrooge in Dickens' *A Christmas Carol* as an illustration.

In that story Scrooge has several visits from spirits, and this leads to his transformation. On Christmas morning he acquires a new vision for how he should treat his fellow man, and then he generously carries out that vision with his employee's family, his own nephew and the charitable foundations in his city. Moody suggests that all of us need to bring our enlightened insights back to our relationships with others, and apply our new wisdom even if it is difficult.[75]

 Moody instructs us that after having the privilege of a spiritual awakening of some kind, it can be tempting for anyone to go into a state that appears holier than thou. When people choose this haughty attitude they may snub others, consider themselves to be the chosen people, and essentially look down their noses at the other mere mortals they have to tolerate. Moody suggests that this attitude is incongruous with the final culminating stage of faith that he calls "The Return". Rather, Moody explains that this ought to be a time of kindness, compassion, and searching for the good in others. It may not be easy, but this could be a phase of life guided by humility and wisdom rather than an attitude of dominion over other people. In the aftermath of a transcendental experience, "The Return" is when a person can freely choose to figure out how to be useful and loving to others.

In a similar vein, Swedenborg teaches that the Lord never compels a person to accept what flows into her from a spiritual experience, but instead leads her gently, keeping her in freedom, and bending her towards finding ways to be good to other people.[76]

So every time that I "Returned" from my spiritual pilgrimages in France, England or Israel, I have to keep checking my attitude whenever ideas of superiority creep into my thoughts. It can be incredibly tempting to give in to love of my

MARY MAGDALENE AS SHE TRIES TO TOUCH THE GARMENT OF JESUS
JERUSALEM, ISRAEL

MARY MAGDALENE AS SHE PREACHES TO EMPEROR TIBERIUS
JERUSALEM, ISRAEL

MARY MAGDALENE'S RELICS IN A CHANDELIER
JERUSALEM, ISRAEL

own intelligence, but I have to pull out those feelings and ideas. Consider the metaphor of a garden: ideas of superiority appear in the mind much like nasty weeds pop up in a garden. Weed pulling is essential before I can go about planting flowers in a beautiful garden. The planting of new flowers corresponds to me taking the initiative to serve others in my roles as a professor, mother, wife, and psychologist. First I must pull out the weeds that represent negative thoughts, and then I can add the flowers that represent my kind behavior. I am still working on applying this idea in my personal life, as I "Return" to my current relationships. It is ongoing.

Moody's fifth stage of faith that he labels "The Return" is quite similar to Swedenborg's concept of loving the neighbor. Swedenborg tells us that first we should stop thinking negative things and then take the initiative to be kind to others.[77] My choice of the metaphor of a garden is certainly not unique, but it is a powerful symbol to help me remember how to actually live effectively in "The Return" stage.

 I imagine that Mary Magdalene was also experiencing her own version of "The Return" stage. Based on what we read in the canonical Gospels of the *Holy Bible*, we know that she was told to "Return" when Jesus instructed her to go tell others what she had witnessed. We are taught:

> Then Jesus said to them, "Do not be afraid. Go and tell my brothers to go to Galilee; there they will see me." (*Holy Bible*, Matthew 28: 10)

> Jesus said . . . "Go instead to my brothers and tell them, I am ascending to my Father and your Father, to my God and your God." (*Holy Bible*, John 20: 17)[78]

After having this heavenly contact with Him while He was ascending to heaven, Mary Magdalene hears that she needs to "Return" to the brethren. Following this intense moment of her spiritual vision of the resurrection and her reception of genuine truths, she went back to talk to the men and women, knowing there was a chance that they might not believe her at all. I can guess that she might have been tempted to be frustrated with these doubtful disciples. She had just had a spiritual awakening, and people might not think she was telling the truth! In the *Holy Bible*, we read:

> So the women hurried away from the tomb, afraid yet filled with joy, and ran to tell His disciples. (*Holy Bible*, Matthew 28: 8)

> And she went and told them that had been with Him, as they mourned and wept. And they, when they had heardthat He was alive, and had been seen of her, believed not." (*Holy Bible*, Mark 16: 10 - 11)

> When they came back from the tomb, they told all these things to the Eleven and to all the others. It was Mary Magdalene, Joanna, Mary the mother of James, and the

others with them who told this to the apostles. But they did not believe the women, because their words seemed to them like nonsense. (*Holy Bible*, Luke 24: 9 - 11)

Mary Magdalene went to the disciples with the news: "I have seen the Lord!" And she told them that He had said these things to her . . . . Now Thomas, one of the Twelve, was not with the disciples when Jesus came. So the other disciples told him, "We have seen the Lord!" But he said to them, "Unless I see the nail marks in his hands and put my finger where the nails were, and put my hand into his side, I will not believe." (*Holy Bible*, John 20: 18 - 25)[79]

Although there are variations in these four canonical Gospels, we see that in several of the accounts of Mary Magdalene's "Return" to the other people that most doubted her testimony. It must have been such an incredible story that it took time and further evidence for them to accept it. But Mary Magdalene seems to have already been convinced and was now Returning to help them understand. Jesus does visibly appear to these devoted followers several times over the next 40 days, and speaks to them directly. Gradually they accept the idea of His ascension, and then they are also engaged in telling others the good news of heaven. The spread of Christianity begins!

According to a modern theological scholar from Harvard University, Dr. Karen King, we can also learn about this era from the ancient document called the *Gospel of Mary*.[80] This 1700 year old document was first found in Egypt in 1896, and then two additional copies of it were found in the 20th century. In it, Mary Magdalene is described as an Apostle to the Apostles.

Apparently, Mary Returned from her encounter with Jesus while He was ascending and completely understood what it meant. Even though the male disciples were often fearful or doubting, she completely believed. She reassured and comforted them as they gradually took up the responsibility of spreading the good news to others. In the Gospel of Mary there are indications that some of the male disciples were jealous of her

MARY MAGDALENE TELLS THE BRETHREN, PAINTING BY WERNER

MARY MAGDALENE TELLS THE BRETHREN, TROYES, FRANCE

enlightenment, which continued to come in visions directly from Jesus to her alone. But even then she is kind and encouraging to them all, as described in this ancient account. She seems to minister to them as she inspires them to courageously carry out the mission. She never sounds condescending, only compassionate and encouraging.[81]

The *Gospel of Mary* is not included in the canonical Gospels of the *Holy Bible*, so I am left wondering whether it is a valid source. It is often called one the Gnostic texts. Recall that in an earlier chapter I summarized the criteria often used by Christian historians to determine a document's validity:

* The older the document, the better.
* The more independent sources of the same ideas, the better.
* If it "cuts against the grain" of predictable ideas, it is less likely to be a forgery.
* New ideas from documents should be considered in the context of previously accepted ideas.[82]

Using Ehrman's criteria to evaluate this document as historical evidence, the *Gospel of Mary* is certainly valuable because it is old. Experts consider it to have been written early in the 2nd century AD. We are fortunate that the *Gospel of Mary* was found and then preserved and translated. According to King, three independent copies of the document have been discovered, which increases its validity, even if none is a complete copy. The *Gospel of Mary* seems to "cut against the grain" in that it portrays Mary Magdalene in a leading role among the apostles. She is Jesus' favorite. This is not the same picture we imagine when we read the works of Roman Catholic theologians. They emphasize the roles of Peter and Paul, and then they established an exclusively male clergy for centuries. Perhaps the Pope invented the story of Mary Magdalene being a sinner to discredit her. But the *Gospel of Mary* describes her in a completely different role from that of a sinner. She is the favorite follower of Jesus, and is nurturing the other apostles during their difficulties.

Finally, the *Gospel of Mary* ought to be considered in the context of previously accepted ideas. This could be analyzed in many ways. In my opinion, it is a story of the life of the apostles in the months after the resurrection. I choose to believe this story more than other non-Gospel books in the Catholic version of the *Holy Bible*, such as Acts or Corinthians. I love how the *Gospel of Mary* includes a description of Mary Magdalene as a woman who was committed to learning about Divine teachings as well as providing comfort to other people in her life. She personifies someone who is trying to live the Two Great Commandments, which are to love the Lord and love the neighbor. This is why she is such a powerful role model for me.[83]

I acknowledge that we are each free to decide whether there is any validity to the *Gospel of Mary*, and I respect you, the reader, to decide for yourself.

THEOLOGICAL TOOL

Emanuel Swedenborg, the 18th century theologian, offers an explanation of the canonical Gospels of the *Holy Bible*, but not the *Gospel of Mary*. Swedenborg focuses on the correspondence of the words of Jesus as He was ascending. Jesus instructed Mary Magdalene to go and tell the brothers. Although we can take this part of the story literally, Swedenborg says it is even more useful for our own spiritual growth to discover what this phrase corresponds to at a spiritual level. He says that the internal meaning of the phrase "go tell the brothers" is that we are to go and be with men and women who are in the good of charity. This means that not only was Mary Magdalene instructed to go be with people who are full of goodness when they are being charitable, but we ought to do the same. In a sense, Jesus Christ is also talking directly to each of us. He is saying that it is helpful for our own spiritual growth for us to look for the kindness in others, and then encourage and enjoy that goodness in them. It is like looking for the positive aspects of other people, while acknowledging that all goodness that we see in people actually originates from God.[84]

 Swedenborg's perspective helps me comprehend the importance of this part of the story of Mary Magdalene. With this view in mind, it is not about a competition between the genders of the apostles and all the ramifications of that political struggle. If I buy into this correspondence of the story, I can choose to apply it to my own social and spiritual life. I actually think it sounds similar to Moody's description of "The Return" after a spiritual awakening. Both Moody and Swedenborg encourage us to enjoy our transcendent experiences, and then go look for other people, seek out their goodness and encourage it. I like to call this spiritual action.

PSYCHOLOGICAL TOOL

Dr. Mary Belenky is the psychologist who focuses on feminine ways of learning and understanding. She and her colleagues describe "Received Knowledge", "Subjective Inner Knowledge", "Procedural Separate Knowledge", "Procedural Connected Knowledge", and finally "Constructed Knowledge". Belenky explains that "Constructed Knowledge" involves a woman's efforts to synthesize all that she has learned from others, from her own inner reflections, and from her separate and connected understanding. It is a complex process of integrating all these competing messages into a unique whole. This can lead to her experiencing mature feminine wisdom, partly based on womanly intuition.[85]

 Belenky tells us that it is useful for a woman to pull apart her different ways of knowing what she knows so she can analyze and appreciate the ideas. I think of this as deconstructing and then reconstructing what she knows. Belenky explains that a woman can consider all the sources of information, and then weave these ways of knowing together into a cohesive whole once she is a mature adult. I am very grateful to Belenky and her colleagues, as she has filled in a gap in the psychological literature that previously had focused more on

male ways of thinking. She and Dr. Carol Gilligan paid more attention to the ways women think than any previous published psychologists in the western world. They inspired dozens of others to stop and consider how women may cognitively differ from men. I also enjoy using this feminine psychological model as I try to understand Mary Magdalene.

However, I don't think that these psychologists of feminine knowledge go quite far enough. They tend to avoid the topic of women learning genuine truths from God. They spend most of their efforts on describing and naming ways that women learn from their intuition or from expert humans. But Belenky never addresses spiritual transformation or enlightened awakenings as a way of knowing. She just avoids examining this key aspect of life.

Looking further, I do find one solitary acknowledgement of spiritual understanding. Approximately a decade after Belenky published *Women's Ways of Knowing* she wrote a sequel along with some other psychologists.[86] In this later publication, *Knowledge, Difference and Power: Essays Inspired by Women's Ways of Knowing*, there is an essay by Dr. Nancy Goldberger.[87] Goldberger devotes one page to acknowledging that perhaps Belenky was doing a disservice to women by implying that anyone who receives doctrine from the Divine is acting like a passive, powerless child relying too much on "Received Knowledge". Goldberger explains that perhaps there is a qualitative difference between "Received Knowledge" which is un-reflected knowledge accepted directly from a human expert, compared to a woman's mature reception of guidance from God. This psychologist suggests that adult women who receive this type of spiritual knowledge may view God as more of a collaborator than an authoritarian tyrant stating commandments. She indicates that the mature adult is actually in freedom.

In this scholarly book of over 450 pages claiming to be all about women's wisdom, there is only one page even hinting that women may learn something valuable from a Divine source. I would argue that psychology helps us name some of our cognitive experiences, but these secular authors do not address them all, and perhaps leave out the most important ones. So I think there are limits to using this psychological theory when explaining Mary Magdalene's experiences of witnessing the resurrection, receiving genuine truth, and then going to tell others. We need to find more tools.

In contrast to the efforts of Belenky and her colleagues to describe women's cognition, there are other psychologists who describe the various aspects of emotion. Recall that Erikson is the developmental psychologist who offers a theory of the eight stages of emotional crises people usually experience across the lifespan. He focuses on human struggles that involve feelings of trust, autonomy, initiative, competence, identity, intimacy, generativity, and integrity.[88]

Recently I have been trying to apply Erikson's theory in my analysis of Mary Magdalene's experiences, but it does not quite work either. We only learn about her as an adult, but she inevitably had childhood and adolescent struggles with trust, autonomy, initiative, competence and identity. Certainly, if she had seven demons invading her body, that must have been very painful and confusing! But then Jesus cast out those demons so she could feel her emotions as her own, thus confirming one aspect of her identity.

Some of those same difficulties were probably revisited involving conflicts about trust, competence and identity after the resurrection. These conflicts are illustrated in her interactions with the male disciples, according to the *Gospel of Mary*. Since no one is certain about the validity of this source, I turn my attention to what she felt according to the canonical-Gospels of the *Holy Bible*. Apparently she felt fear, worry, joy, and serenity all on Easter morning. Those are specific emotions that she experienced within the context of her overall struggle for generativity and integrity. Erikson tells us that most adults struggle to figure out how to help the next generation (generativity) and how to live according to some guiding principles (integrity). Erikson claims that elderly adults spend most of their time looking in reverse as they ask themselves if they have lived in integrity or do they feel despair for wasting their lives.

When I compare Erikson's theory to Belenky's theory, they seem like yin and yang. Erikson addresses the emotional aspect of life and Belenky focuses on cognition. People both feel and think, yet each of these psychologists chose to focus in on just one aspect of life. I think we need to study both aspects and examine how they complement each other in the spiritually mature adult. This can help us appreciate Mary Magdalene's life, as well as our own.

But just as I critiqued Belenky's work for avoiding the discussion of how women acquire genuine truths, I also see that Erikson avoids the topic of how people acquire genuine love. Erikson leaves out any description of how a person may be looking forward to a future afterlife. So again, this psychological theory is a good beginning for explaining human development, but in the end it is an inadequate tool. We need more.

 This is where I find it useful to supplement psychological theories with philosophical and theological ideas I learn from reading Swedenborg. He discusses how these two aspects, emotions and cognition, are present in every normal adult. If we choose to spiritually grow, we are more likely to humbly acknowledge that all positive emotions and thoughts originate from God. The more we feel positive emotions flowing through us, the more we are flourishing with goodness from God. And the more we comprehend positive thoughts coming to us, the more we are enlightened with truth from God. We have the joy of sensing goodness and truth within us, but we do not take credit for being the source of these qualities. Then, if we take this a step further, whenever we attempt to combine the complementary aspects of goodness and truth, we could envision the metaphor of a marriage. Marriage corresponds to this synthesis of our most positive thoughts and feelings.[89]

For example, it appears that Mary Magdalene had her spiritual eyes opened and that Jesus presented her with genuine truths about the resurrection and the afterlife. She felt Divine truth entering her mind and she received this cognitive enlightenment. But this was not just an intellectual experience. In addition, we are told that she experienced the emotion of great joy. So both her thoughts and her emotions were engaged at that moment. I sense that she was "marrying" these truths and joys together into a totally transcendent experience.

Swedenborg teaches that just as a physical marriage often leads to the birth of children, the symbol of marriage corresponds to how a person can produce spiritual offspring. The best spiritual offspring are our creative efforts to serve others. Our unique spiritual offspring are visible in the useful services we choose to perform for other people, especially with a positive, humble attitude.

Mary Magdalene could have kept all this Divine truth and goodness to herself and retreated to a mountaintop by herself, but she didn't. She immediately shared it with others. So it is likely that she experienced an internal "marriage" of goodness and truth. Then she experienced the "spiritual offspring" of telling others about the resurrection, and encouraging goodness in other people. I like to identify this useful activity of "telling the brothers" as her spiritual actions.

This Swedenborgian description of the union of thinking and feeling and then acting sounds somewhat similar to Moody's theory of the *Five Stages of the Soul* and Fowler's theory of the *Stages of Faith*. Moody calls his final stage of spiritual growth "The Return" and Fowler names his final stage "Universalizing Faith". Based on these theological and philosophical perspectives, I can appreciate a synthesized description of our spiritual growth. I understand that in the most mature state of spiritual growth we can experience the reception of universal genuine truths, a deep love of what is good, and an intense desire to act and serve other people. Although these philosophers, psychologists and theologians use different words they seem to be harmoniously describing the same final stage of spiritual growth![90]

Swedenborg also offers some additional descriptions of stages of faith as further explanation. One of his descriptions involves four stages across the lifespan:

* 1) "The first phase is when our behavior follows other people's instructions.
* 2) The second is when our behavior is our own, and our intellect restrains us.
* 3) The third is when our will pushes our intellect and our intellect restrains our will.
* 4) The fourth is when our behavior is deliberate and purposeful".[91]

This description is another way of explaining how we can mature, if we choose, using our intellect and our will (emotions). At first we just follow along in a child-like manner. Then we learn how to control our own behavior. I think the third stage is quite interesting, perhaps because I can relate to it as an aging adult. Swedenborg says that as adults, we push and restrain our thoughts and feelings through moral and spiritual struggles. But if we eventually "marry" our best thoughts and feelings in an integrated manner, we then behave deliberately and with purpose. We draw on truth and goodness from God, but we are responsible for how we combine them and then behave with other people. At this stage of maturity, we are deliberate and purposeful about our actions.

I find this combination of psychological, philosophical and theological ideas very helpful as I venture on my own spiritual journey. Just I am gaining confidence as a solitary international traveler looking for sacred sites in foreign countries, I am also gaining confidence about my spiritual journey. I need to keep acknowledging that truth and goodness did not come from me . . . they originate from God. My job is to be receptive, synthesize a marriage of good and truth within me, and then take the initiative to act on what I feel and think. This is my transcendent itinerary.

Recently I have been contemplating all these theories and wondering if I could create a simple model like a staircase to help me and others on our spiritual journeys. I decided to focus on the theme of sincerity. Based on theoretical ideas borrowed from Bloom, Maslow, Erikson, Fowler, Belenky, Kohlberg, Gilligan, Moody, and Swedenborg, I suddenly started writing down my own model. Since then I have revised this theory a few times, and here is the most recent version. I suggest you read the hierarchical model from the bottom up, like climbing a staircase, and then privately contemplate your own level of sincerity in your daily thoughts, feelings and actions. You might vary day by day, but with deliberate and purposeful work, you can spiritually grow and function at the highest levels of sincerity more often. I trust that this experience will bring you great joy as you feel the Lord flowing through you.

My Hierarchical Model of Sincerity

7) Sincerely committing to love God
   and people.
6) Purposefully willing to shun evils and do
   good actions.
5) Deliberately planning to follow what is
   believed to be true.
4) Reluctantly and insincerely complying with
   moral and spiritual guidelines.
3) Occasionally doing spontaneous moral thinking,
   feeling or acting.
2) Conformity, by simply being willing to obey rules
   and laws of authorities.
1) Unaware of civil, moral or spiritual truths, so cannot
   be held accountable for them.[92]

Although I must be careful not to spiritually judge anyone, including Mary Magdalene, I am speculating that her thinking, feeling and acting around the time of the resurrection illustrate some of the highest levels of spiritual growth that a person can experience. Her actions seemed deliberate and purposeful when she did what Jesus instructed her to do. In the literal sense she obeyed and went to tell the brothers about Jesus rising from the tomb. But in the internal sense she united her Divinely inspired feelings and thoughts, and then deliberately acted with the purpose of supporting the goodness she saw in everyone she met. She seems so sincere.

Mary Magdalene was spiritually aware, spiritually accepting and spiritually acting. We can be this sincere in our lives, if we choose.

CHAPEL WINDOW, PAINTING BY WERNER
ABBEY OF FONTANY, FRANCE

CHAPTER 7

Finding Mary Magdalene

During my visit to Israel I am thrilled to finally see the sacred sites in Jerusalem and around the Sea of Galilee. In Jerusalem I learn that the current "Old City" is about a square mile, surrounded by a medieval wall built after the Crusades of the Middle Ages. Jerusalem has been conquered and destroyed so many times that it has been very difficult for archaeologists and theologians to determine the exact locations of sacred events. Perhaps the rubble has accumulated from so many burnings and demolitions that the actual sites are deep below the surface.

Then there is the problem of shared space. There is currently a tense agreement between the Islamic people, the Jews and the Christians about how to share the Old City of Jerusalem. They each think that religiously significant events happened in Jerusalem and they want shrines to honor them. But they are in the same location! There are claims that Abraham almost crucified his son at the same spot that the prophet Muhammad was lifted up to heaven, which is the same spot where Solomon had built a temple. So over the past thousand years or so people have divided the city up into sections and have built homes, cathedrals, temples, mosques, and commercial zones in very tightly secured zones. I notice security guards with very big machine guns slung over their shoulders, and they are everywhere to make sure religious fanatics do not interfere with each others' spiritual rituals. I see many of the astonishing Jewish and Islamic sites in Jerusalem, and hear people in devoted worship, but will just tell you the story of my walk through the most sacred avenue of Christian history: the Via Dolorosa.[93]

The Via Dolorosa is Latin for the "Way of the Cross or Suffering". The leaders from the Roman Catholic, the Greek Orthodox, the Armenian Christian, and the Coptic Egyptian Churches have come to an agreement. They established this avenue winding through the Christian Quarter so pilgrims can walk in the footsteps of Jesus where He struggled to His crucifixion. Today it is a steep journey on pavement and cobblestones, marked by the 14 Stations of the Cross. (The 15th is the Lord's resurrection.)[94]

VIA DOLOROSA
JERUSALEM, ISRAEL

	...s is condemned to death
	...esus receives His Cross
III	Jesus falls the first time under His Cross
IV	Jesus meets Mary His Mother
V	Simon of Cyrene helps Jesus to carry His Cross
VI	Veronica wipes the face of Jesus
VII	Jesus falls the second time
VIII	Jesus speaks to the women of Jerusalem
IX	Jesus falls the third time
X	Jesus is stripped of His garments
XI	Jesus is nailed to the Cross
XII	Jesus dies on the Cross
XIII	Jesus is taken down from the Cross
XIV	Jesus is laid in the Tomb

STATIONS OF THE CROSS, VIA DOLOROSA, JERUSALEM, ISRAEL

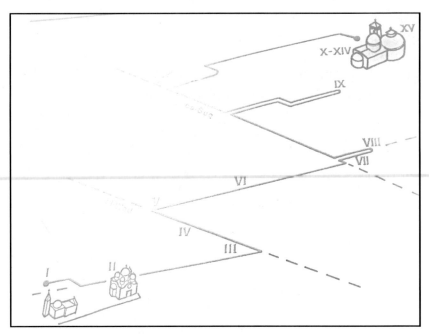

ROUTE OF VIA DOLOROSA, JERUSALEM, ISRAEL

LION'S GATE
JERUSALEM, ISRAEL

WERNER TOUCHING THE SACRED WALL, VIA DOLOROSA, JERUSALEM, ISRAEL

VIA DOLOROSA
JERUSALEM, ISRAEL

145

MUSLIM QUARTER ON THE LEFT, CHRISTIAN QUARTER ON THE RIGHT
VIA DOLOROSA, JERUSALEM, ISRAEL

VIA DOLOROSA, JERUSALEM, ISRAEL

ALLEGED BIRTHPLACE OF VIRGIN MARY, JERUSALEM, ISRAEL

TRIAL OF JESUS, VIA DOLOROSA, JERUSALEM, ISRAEL

JESUS TAKES UP THE CROSS
VIA DOLOROSA, JERUSALEM, ISRAEL

WOODEN CROSSES AVAILABLE
FOR PILGRIMS TO CARRY,
VIA DOLOROSA, JERUSALEM, ISRAEL

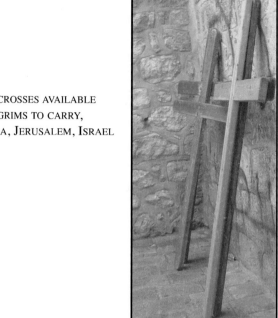

PILGRIMS CARRY A CROSS
VIA DOLOROSA, JERUSALEM, ISRAEL

MARY THE MOTHER GREETS JESUS, VIA DOLOROSA, JERUSALEM, ISRAEL

SIMON GREETS JESUS, VIA DOLOROSA, JERUSALEM, ISRAEL

These stations are loosely based on the canonical Gospels of the *Holy Bible*. They offer a tangible method for a pilgrim to contemplate what Jesus may have experienced as He was tried, condemned, made to carry His cross up the hill, put to death, and buried. Current pilgrims can walk up the steep hill to Calvary, even carrying a wooden cross to simulate the event. I walk for hours along the Via Dolorosa with people of varying ages and nationalities. On my pilgrimage, I notice the great emphasis on the Virgin Mary. I see the supposed location of her birthplace, and where she may have comforted Jesus.

Wait a minute! I was stunned to see that another female was mentioned at one of the stations: Veronica. I checked my tiny portable *Holy Bible* that I had in my pocket. There is no mention of a woman named Veronica in the canonical Gospels! Who was she? The signs tell me that she wiped off tears, blood and sweat from Jesus' face while He carried the cross. But this is a literary fantasy and no one around me seems to be commenting on this detail. They just read and keep walking. I mention this discrepancy in the story to my guide, but he says nothing and just shrugs his shoulders. The religious leaders have apparently invented this character, named her Veronica, and inserted her into this sacred story! I can hardly believe it.[95]

 Then it dawns on me. I realize that Mary Magdalene was never actually mentioned at any of the Stations of the Cross. According to the canonical Gospels, we know she was there, grieving for Him along with the Virgin Mary. Why did the church leaders leave Mary Magdalene out and insert Veronica? Why didn't anyone else seem annoyed about this manipulation of the Gospels? I sigh and keep on walking.

At the eighth station, the literature says that Jesus spoke to the women of Jerusalem.[96] Which women? Doesn't say. Keep walking. It is rainy and the cobblestones are slippery. When we finally reach the highest point on the hill there is an odd sort of combination of buildings called the Cathedral of the Holy Sepulcher. In there are the final Stations of the Cross, where Jesus was supposedly nailed to the cross, taken down, and laid in the tomb. Then we approach the sacred site where we believe He rose from the tomb. I am standing where Mary Magdalene encountered angels, the earthquake and the ascending Lord. I am in awe!

 This is a busy place and certainly not a location for serene meditation. I was overcome with the bombardment of stimuli. Hundreds of people are coming and going through the zones and looking at the mosaics and paintings that illustrate the last hours of Jesus' earthly life. Guards push us along in a herd and there is no place to sit and contemplate it all. The space in there is strictly divided up between the four or five church denominations who decorate the zones with their religious items, then spontaneously preach, hold services or sing. There is a tense, competitive agreement between these religious sects, governed by strict laws. The regulations concern which churches can manage the zones where they think the cross was pounded into the rock, the mystical marble slab that was positioned over the platform where Jesus' body was placed, and the site of the sepulcher. I can actually see the lines between the zones and the very different types of religious decorations hanging in each space.[97]

I hear that there is only one entrance into this Cathedral of the Holy Sepulcher and no Christian may hold the key. It has been legally entrusted to a Muslim family for centuries and every morning one of them opens the door. The competition between Christian leaders can become so aggressive that no one can be trusted to get in there early because they might vandalize the sacred zones of the other church sects. Oh, my. Is this what Jesus would have wanted? He told us to love one another. Have we forgotten His message?

CATHEDRAL OF THE HOLY SEPULCHER, VIA DOLOROSA, JERUSALEM, ISRAEL

CATHEDRAL OF THE HOLY SEPULCHER, VIA DOLOROSA, JERUSALEM, ISRAEL

INSIDE THE CATHEDRAL OF THE HOLY SEPULCHER
VIA DOLOROSA, JERUSALEM, ISRAEL

INSIDE GLASS CONTAINER IS THE TOP OF THE STONY HILL
WHERE JESUS WAS CRUCIFIED, VIA DOLOROSA, JERUSALEM, ISRAEL

 In the swirling crowd I try to capture photos of the paintings and mosaic on the walls. I find Mary Magdalene! There are no signs with her name, but I can pick out the familiar images. In the huge mosaic she is illustrated as one of the many people at the foot of the cross, and then helping to carry Jesus to a platform. The Virgin Mary is shown with a halo and she is holding His head, but I am not sure if Mary Magdalene is shown with a halo or not. They are all portrayed as if in deep mourning.

I am a bit confused as I think there are actually three tombs among the sacred sites, because various Christian groups are in dispute about the location of where Jesus was buried. (The Protestants claim it was half a mile away!) I take a photo of the inside of one of them — very dark and only lit with candles. Then on the nearby walls I see some artwork depicting my favorite part of the story: when Mary Magdalene spoke to the ascending Jesus. No signs saying her name, but at least the visual images show the most important scene. No pictures of legends and nothing illustrating her as a penitent sinner. I am thrilled! At least the conflicted church sect leaders here at the Cathedral of the Holy Sepulcher agree to leave out irrelevant images and focus on Jesus telling Mary Magdalene about His ascension.[98]

 I wasn't here hoping for a miracle, but I see people who do. There seems to be a custom of bringing a cloth or piece of paper and rubbing it on the marble slab that is supposed to be directly above where Jesus' body was laid before the burial. I touch the slab but do not partake in rubbing it. I hear that people hope that if they rub it and then bring the cloth to a part of their body that is sick, they might be miraculously cured. I have never actually witnessed this kind of ritual before. It was more specific than the general rituals of pilgrims walking the labyrinth at Chartres. Pilgrims were really hoping to be instantly cured of a disease! Maybe it happens to some people, but no miracles occurred on the day that I was there. I wonder how they handle the disappointments.

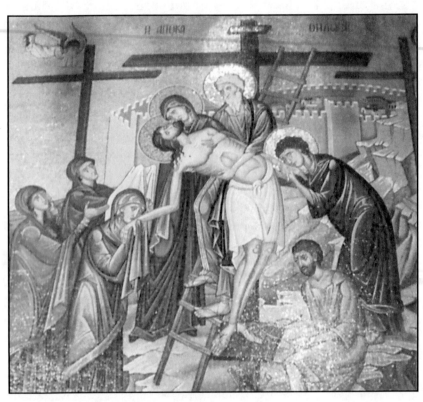

MOSAIC, VIA DOLOROSA, JERUSALEM, ISRAEL

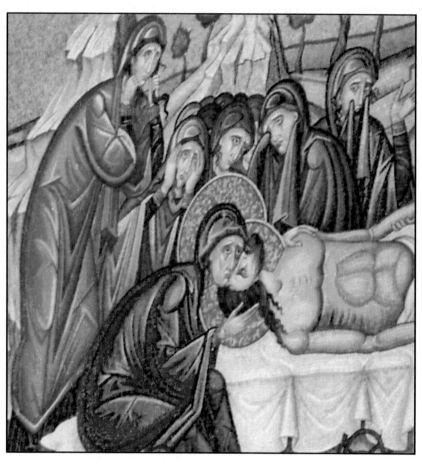

MOSAIC, VIA DOLOROSA, JERUSALEM, ISRAEL

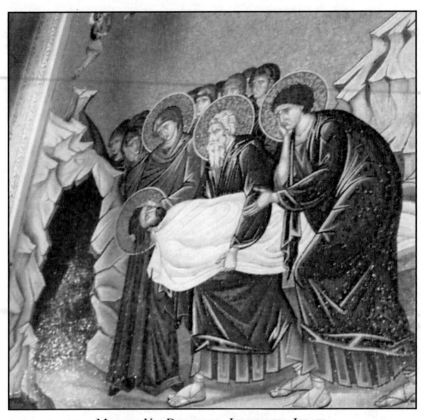

MOSAIC, VIA DOLOROSA, JERUSALEM, ISRAEL

MARBLE SLAB SITUATED OVER SPOT WHERE
HIS BODY WAS LAID AFTER CRUCIFIXION,
VIA DOLOROSA, JERUSALEM, ISRAEL

WERNER TOUCHING THE MARBLE SLAB
JERUSALEM, ISRAEL

PILGRIMS HOPE FOR A MIRACLE
WHEN THEY RUB THE MARBLE SLAB,
JERUSALEM, ISRAEL

CANDLELIT SEPULCHER, VIA DOLOROSA, JERUSALEM, ISRAEL

MARY MAGDALENE MEETS JESUS
VIA DOLOROSA, JERUSALEM, ISRAEL

MARY MAGDALENE MEETS JESUS
VIA DOLOROSA, JERUSALEM, ISRAEL

For many people who travel to Israel, the highlight of their pilgrimage is walking the Via Dolorosa. But for me the best was yet to come. The next two days I spend in the region around the Sea of Galilee. I want to see where Mary was from: Magdala! I was eager to see where Jesus had performed miracles, including casting out her demons. We drive for hundreds of miles through Israel. I see Emmaus, Tiberius, Cana, Nazareth, Capernaum and the location where He gave His Sermon on the Mount. This site is now called the Mt. of Beatitudes and the monks provide a lovely place for meditation from this high location. I see visiting clergy leading pilgrims through worship services and individuals praying in the shrine of the Beatitudes. Compared to the tense, bustling environment in Jerusalem's Cathedral of the Holy Sepulcher, this is heavenly.

I linger here at this serene shrine for a long time. I meditate on the ten blessings, or beatitudes, and feel the comfort of Jesus saying them to me personally. I feel His blessing as I think about my work as a peacemaker when I teach people about conflict resolution skills back at my college. I imagine Mary Magdalene sitting on this very hill listening to Him preach, taking it all in.

Down the hill from this shrine I can see where we think Magdala once existed. Now it is a beautiful rural area known as Migdal, surrounded by the Sea of Galilee, the Mt. of Beatitudes, Capernaum, and the mountains where Jesus may have gone up to pray alone. Magdala means "great" or "magnificent" in the Aramaic language, but in Hebrew it means "tower". Magdala Nunayya means "a tower of fishes", so many scholars conclude that there used to be a tower here where fish were dried and stored along the Sea of Galilee. This is where Jesus probably met Mary Magdalene, as well as many of the disciples who used to be fishermen. Near here, He miraculously fed thousands of followers with just a few fish and loaves of bread. He changed water to wine at the wedding in Cana. He preached in the synagogues and cured the sick. He asked Peter to feed his lambs. He said He would build His church on the rock. It all happened here.[99]

After spending the night in a simple bed and breakfast inn near Migdal, I wake up to see the sunrise over the water where Jesus had walked and calmed the wind many years ago. I decide to read all the stories of His ministry in the four canonical Gospels of the *Holy Bible* while sitting beside the Sea of Galilee. I have no idea how long I sat there reading and watching the sunrise, but it was pure bliss. I re-read the 10 blessings and think about Mary Magdalene. I dislike the ways some people have misused her name and legacy over the centuries, and then I think about the last three blessings:

> "Blessed are they who are persecuted for the sake of righteousness, for theirs is the kingdom of heaven. Blessed are you when they insult you and persecute you and utter every kind of evil against you (falsely) because of me. Rejoice and be glad, for your reward will be great in heaven." (*Holy Bible*, Matthew 5: 10-12)

I like to think of Jesus saying these words about her. She may not even be aware that since she left this earth some people have worshipped her, some have invented stories about her, some have insulted her, some have persecuted her and uttered all kinds of evil and falsities about her. Now I like to think of her as blessed and rejoicing in heaven.

In my Swedenborgian view of heaven, I believe we get to choose wonderful, useful jobs there, and that we enjoy doing them because we love to serve others. So I like to imagine Mary Magdalene there in heaven, full of blessings, and rejoicing as she sincerely does her favorite job. Maybe her job will be to greet new arrivals when they first wake up in heaven, and maybe she gets to tell them the good news. Perhaps she is still telling the brethren, which means she is looking for the goodness in other people and encouraging it. Maybe she will even greet me when I arrive.

SIGN FOR MIGDAL, CURRENT NAME FOR ANCIENT CITY OF MAGDALA
HOME OF MARY MAGDALENE, ISRAEL

MIGDAL, ALONG THE SEA OF GALILEE, ISRAEL

PILGRIMS NEAR THE SEA OF GALILEE, ISRAEL

SITE OF SERMON ON THE MOUNT, MT. OF BEATITUDES, ISRAEL

MONASTERY AT MT. OF BEATITUDES, ISRAEL

MENSA CHRIST =
TABLE OF JESUS CHRIS
ISRAEL

WERNER TOUCHING THE MENSA CHRIST, ISRAEL

SITE OF MIRACLES OF FISH AND BREAD
CHURCH OF HEPTAPEGON, ISRAEL

MOUNTAIN WHERE JESUS MAY HAVE GONE UP TO PRAY, ISRAEL

CHAPEL ON THE ROCK, FOR PETER, SEA OF GALILEE, ISRAEL

CAPERNAUM,
SITE OF MANY MIRACLES
AND SERMONS,
ISRAEL

ANCIENT SYNAGOGUE WHERE JESUS MAY HAVE PREACHED
ISRAEL

CAPERNAUM, ISRAEL

And Jesus said to the man who had
been ill for thirty-eight years,
"Rise, take up your pallet, and walk."
see John 5

SIGN ABOUT JESUS HEALING THE SICK, ISRAEL

SITE OF BAPTISMS, JORDAN RIVER, ISRAEL

JORDAN RIVER, ISRAEL

VIEW OF MIGDAL AND SEA OF GALILEE
PAINTING BY WERNER
ISRAEL

SITE WHERE JESUS WALKS ON THE WATER
SEA OF GALILEE AT SUNRISE
PAINTING BY WERNER
ISRAEL

CONCLUSION

When I grew up in a Christian family and community, most of the Biblical stories I heard included men as their main characters. We learned about Moses, Joseph, Jonah, Noah and Abraham. I saw them in the stained glass windows of the Bryn Athyn Cathedral, which are medieval in style but Swedenborgian in their Biblical interpretations. These male characters each had moments when they heard or saw God and were instructed to go and deliberately do something with great purpose.

It didn't occur to me until midlife that it actually bothered me that there were so few female characters highlighted in the *Holy Bible*. I began searching for female role models, not so I could worship them, but so I could be inspired to grow spiritually in a more feminine way. Mary Magdalene seems more fascinating to me than the Virgin Mary or Eve. Jesus seemed to distance himself from his earthly mother Mary at the end, so I have always wondered why so many people in the Catholic Church set up statues of her and worshipped all the details about the Virgin Mary. In contrast, Eve was infamous for bringing evil into the world.

If I selected the Virgin Mary or Eve I was constantly thinking about how women are too frequently sainted, marginalized or blamed. So I shifted my focus and started to think more deeply about Mary Magdalene. I never thought of her as a saint, but I wanted to know her as a distant friend or mentor. She became my role model.

 When I heard tales, songs and legends of Mary Magdalene that seemed inconsistent with the canonical Gospels, I was even more fascinated. Sometimes I even got angry at how her name was misused. I have been sorting out what I know and feel about her for a very long time; my search has been the most intense in the past decade.

When I learned what the Roman Catholic Pope said about her in 591 AD, I was irritated. That's where that rumor started! But then when I heard how this story about her as a sinner was taken to an extreme by the Irish clergy and nuns at the Magdalen Asylums and Laundries, I was absolutely furious. At least 30,000 Irish girls and young women were captured, enslaved, beaten and sexually abused, all justified under the erroneous legend of Mary Magdalene. This was the clergy's love of dominion gone out of control, and ironically this behavior was the exact opposite of the mercy that Jesus demonstrated with women who had made mistakes.

Watching the documentary film, *The Magdalene Sisters*, was a low point in my research. It was easy for me to reject this view of Mary Magdalene as the repentant sinner. No matter which stained glass window, statue or fresco I see of her portrayed in this role, I disregard all of this artwork portraying her as the repentant sinner.

On another vein of my research I learned about devoted pilgrims who yearn to see her relics, and this has been going on for a thousand years. I saw them in the Gothic cathedrals of France, most notably in Vezalay, Burgundy. I felt in awe of their devotion but I knew I was separate from them as they prayed for grace in front of a bone marked "Reliques de St Marie Madeleine." But when I analyzed the facts, I could not accept the premise that she ever even traveled to France after the resurrection. I am similar to the devoted pilgrims in wanting to know about her as a means of growing spiritually, but I differ in that I choose not to worship her alleged bones. So I respectfully disregard the worship of her relics.

When in Paris, my husband and I enthusiastically visited L'Eglise de la St. Madeleine. This church is a building designed to look like a Roman Temple, and was originally constructed to honor the glory of the French army and remind observers of the late, great, Roman Empire. It was all about power. Later on, the church took it over and dedicated it to Mary Magdalene. While I appreciate this prominent focus on her in the heart of Paris, I was disappointed with the spotlights on a statue of her portrayed as flying up to heaven in the arms of angels. This illustrates their beloved legend that she moved to France, lived in a grotto, and was elevated up daily while she prayed. Although I love to learn about how Mary Magdalene had spiritual encounters with the Divine, this feels like the wrong story to be highlighting. It seems like this is a subtle way of using Mary Magdalene's name to bring glory to the French nation, based on an unsubstantiated legend. So I respectfully disregard this French tale as illustrated in stone at the L'Eglise de la St. Madeleine.

During a recent trip through rural England where I was involved in a wonderful retreat with other Swedenborgian readers, I happened to drive by the world famous Magdalen College of Oxford University. I did not know it at the time, but I later discovered that this is one of the major academic institutions that has adopted Mary Magdalene's name. According to their webpage, the college leaders are much more interested in an accurate account of their college history than they are of the history of their namesake. They highlight all their founding fathers in the 15th century and their famous alumni who have attended their college. But there is almost nothing provided to readers about who Mary Magdalene actually was in the story of Jesus Christ, even though they have an active Christian chapel on their campus. So, I am saddened by this error of omission, and I respectfully disregard Oxford's Magdalen College as a reliable source of information about her.

In 2003, millions of people began to read Brown's detective novel *The DaVinci Code*, or later on they may have seen the movie. I joined in and was captivated by the story, but it raised dozens of serious questions in my mind. I have also read modern novels by Kathleen McGowan and feel the same way about her assertions. Since then, with the help of scholars such as Ehrman, King and Newman I separated the fiction from the history. This investigation led me to conclude that there is absolutely no evidence in either the canonical Gospels of the *Holy Bible* or other ancient Gospels to support either Brown's or McGowan's premise that Jesus had a wife and child. Therefore, I believe that there is no sacred bloodline. As a result, I do not believe anyone can claim that they are physical descendants of Jesus and Mary Magdalene. I also doubt the credibility of such claims in the Mormon Church, even though they are known for keeping careful track of ancestry. While I enjoy a great detective story, I am discouraged that the authors of *The DaVinci Code* and *The Book of Love* seem more interested in questionable legends about Mary Magdalene than telling the world about the true story of her life with Jesus Christ. So, I respectfully disregard most of the details about Mary Magdalene in these modern works of historical fiction.

Once we peel away these distracting legends, tales, novels and mistaken images of her, what's left? I think it is the best story of all.

Mary Magdalene was not a saint, the wife of Jesus, a prostitute, an adulterer, or a figure flying up to heaven in the arms of angels from her French grotto. She was an ordinary woman who witnessed extraordinary things. She came to Jesus' empty tomb, talked with brightly clothed angels, saw an earthquake, was instructed not to touch Him while He was ascending, and then was urged by Jesus to go tell the brothers about the resurrection.

I am assuming that she was afraid, worried, joyful, trusting, serene and kind. I interpret this to mean that she was spiritually aware, accepting and acting on what she learned directly from God.

With the use of psychological and philosophical theories I have provided several perspectives for analyzing her life. Belenky describes how women think, while Erikson offers a theory for how people deal with emotional struggles. Bloom presents his taxonomy of the Affective Domain, and Maslow gives us the Hierarchy of Needs. Gilligan tells us that women are motivated by the care they bring to relationships, while Kohlberg emphasizes how people can reach the highest moral level by searching for universal truth. Moody and Fowler are some of the few modern authors who actually discuss stages of spiritual growth. Although their terminology differs from each other, they agree that the final stage of spiritual growth involves embracing genuine truths and applying them to life in positive relationships with other people. I concur with some elements of these theories of spiritual growth and offer my own Theory of the Hierarchy of Sincerity. I believe that it is when we are functioning most sincerely that we receive truth and goodness from God, and then we can respond with love to God and other people.

As far as I can tell, few modern authors have brought Swedenborg's theological perspective to an understanding of Mary Magdalene. If we use this lens we can see the internal sense of her experiences on what we call Easter morning. (For a list of some Swedenborgian sermons and articles about Easter and *The DaVinci Code*, see the List of References.)

Mary Magdalen met brightly clothed angels, which corresponds to her spiritual eyes being opened by God. At that moment she was ready to receive the genuine truths being presented to her. She saw an earthquake and knew that this meant that an enormous change was about to happen in the state of the church: Christianity was born with the new awareness of the afterlife as demonstrated by Jesus' ascension. She met Jesus as He was ascending and He instructed her to not touch Him. She could understand that His human self (Jesus) was uniting with His Divine Self (Father in heaven). They are one in the name of the Lord God Jesus Christ. There is only one God and she felt confident in this truth, and that He truly was the promised Messiah. Then she was urged to tell the brothers, and she comprehended this to mean that she must go back to all of His followers and encourage goodness in everyone she met.

In addition to these direct Biblical interpretations of the essential story of Mary Magdalene, I brought in other concepts from Swedenborg's Writings. I summarized his description of the four stages of spiritual growth, and the correspondence of the union or "marriage" of our most positive thoughts and feelings. This "marriage" is essential as we weave together our wisdom and will, giving credit to God as the source of all that is genuinely true and good. The "spiritual offspring" of this union can lead to our unique actions of serving other people in our lives as a way to give back to God. There is an unlimited number of ways that we can serve others; if we do it with a sincere and grateful heart we will flourish and feel part of something bigger than ourselves. This is like experiencing the community of heaven, even while we are still on earth.

Although I do not accept the concept of the sacred bloodline as stated by Dan Brown, Kathleen McGowan, the Mormon Church or anyone who tells the French legend, I do appreciate how people long to see a spiritual union. But I believe it is a serious mistake to use the literary fantasy of a marriage between Jesus and Mary Magdalene to fulfill this longing for a sacred union. Instead, I encourage people to learn about the "marriage of goodness and truth" that each person can form at an individual, spiritual level. Swedenborg tells us that our most positive thoughts and feelings originate from God, but we can choose to experience them and form them together in our souls. When we do this sincerely, we sense the Lord's truth coming into our intellect and His goodness coming into our will. We learn to love how truth and goodness work in unity and help us grow spiritually. We experience the joy of "spiritual offspring" in the form of unique actions we choose to perform as we serve our neighbors. The more we long for this kind of sacred marriage, the less we go astray and get sidetracked into thinking false ideas.

I thoroughly enjoyed learning about Mary Magdalene at both the literal and internal levels. I loved traveling across America, England, France and Israel to see sacred sites related to her legacy. I hear there are other shrines, colleges and cathedrals dedicated to her in England, Asia and America, and maybe I will visit them all someday. Although it has been a challenge to gather up information and sort it all out, it has been an engaging process. The Greeks might say I am experiencing a thelema type of love, as I am passionately involved in this endeavor.

I wish the essential tale of Mary Magdalene on Easter morning was more well known and not crowded out by all the mistaken literary fantasies and legends illustrated in literature, musical productions and artwork. If I can be just one voice, let me use it to bring attention to the essential story of Mary Magdalene and what it corresponds to in our spiritual maturation.

Soon I will finish my sabbatical and return to my classroom to teach students at Bryn Athyn College. As Moody says, this will be my "Return." This is a liberal arts college and the faculty there love to draw students' attention to the Swedenborgian perspective of life. The faculty are also involved in applying Swedenborgian ideas to our particular areas of expertise. Recently our college President, Dr. Kristin King, stated that among the college faculty, "intellectual inquiry is valued, and new applications and new thought, based on sound research and argument, are encouraged . . . . It is a place where new questions are posed, new research uncovered, new findings made, new applications explored."[100]

My academic areas are psychology and theology. I have appreciated this time off from teaching to pose these new interdisciplinary questions, and to explore this new application of the Swedenborgian perspective. I searched for the essential story of Mary Magdalene and found what her story means for my spiritual development.

I can recall her story and think about my own process of:

* Searching for truth.
* Being ready to receive it.
* Noticing changes in the church on earth.
* Pondering about the meaning of Jesus' ascension and glorification.
* Then looking for goodness in other people and encouraging it.

I will strive not to:

* Use the name of Mary Magdalene and then ignore her essential story as they do at Oxford University.
* Misuse her name when discussing the sinning women in the *Holy Bible* as the Catholic Pope and clergy did.
* Misuse her name to dominate other people as the Irish clergy did in the Magdalene Laundries.
* Misuse her name to elevate the glory of one nation as they do in France.
* Misuse her name by emphasizing questionable legends about her as Brown and McGowen did.

As I try to "tell the brethren" and search for goodness in others; I am full of gratitude for:

* The Eastern Orthodox Church for never conflating her name with the sinning women in the Gospels, and for preserving the story of her role on Easter.
* The artists of the medieval and renaissance eras who painted exquisite images of the resurrection story.
* The scholars such as Karen King and Bart Ehrman who carefully explained the non-canonical Gospels that included information about Mary Magdalene.
* The Russian Romanov family who bought land on the Mount of Olives and built my favorite shrine dedicated to the memory of Mary Magdalene.
* Emanuel Swedenborg for serving as a scribe to the Lord's revelation and providing us with spiritual interpretations of the resurrection story.
* Swedenborgian clergymen and women, such as Ray Silverman and Susannah Currie, who have written about Mary Magdalene from this enlightened perspective.
* Stained glass window designers of the Bryn Athyn Cathedral and Glencairn Museum for adopting the style of the Gothic European cathedrals, but basing their resurrection images on the canonical Gospels of the Holy Bible.
* Mary Magdalene and all the other apostles who bravely followed Jesus.

In conclusion, I plan to continue to draw inspiration from her wonderful roles as a female friend, follower and apostle of the teachings of the Lord God Jesus Christ. I have searched for and found Mary Magdalene, and she gives me courage.

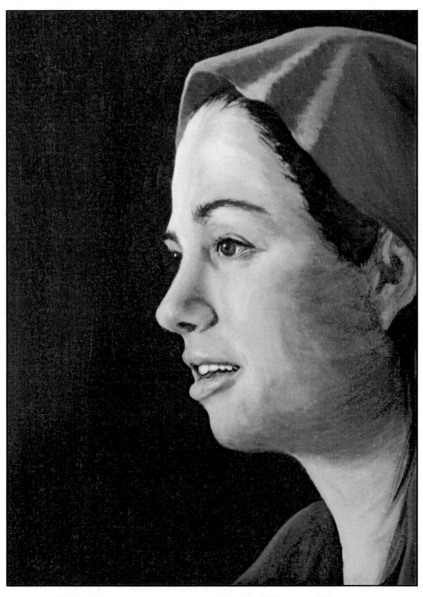

MARY MAGDALENE IS CONFIDENT THAT HE IS THE MESSIAH
PAINTING BY WERNER

MARY MAGDALENE AND ANOTHER WOMAN MEET AN ANGEL
GLENCAIRN MUSEUM, WINDOWS BY HYATT
BRYN ATHYN, PA, USA

MARY MAGDALENE AND JESUS
GLENCAIRN MUSEUM, WINDOWS BY HYATT
BRYN ATHYN, PA, USA

About the Author

Dr. Soni Soneson Werner is a Swedenborgian Developmental Psychologist. She currently teaches psychology and interpersonal communication skills at Bryn Athyn College to undergraduates and graduate theological students. Soni is married to Dr. Neil Werner and they have two grown daughters.

ENDNOTES

1. Diamant (1997). Tells the story of the children of Israel from a sister's perspective.
2. Moody (1997).
3. www.catholictradition.org/Saints/signs2.htm
4. Cohen (date unknown), p. 63.
5. David (1964) hymn #217.
6. Fowler (1981).
7. Vatican II was the result of discussions among Catholic leadership. One result is that there was more allowance for laity to read the Bible. Back in the 1300's, the Catholic Church absolutely forbid the laity to read the Bible in their native languages, but the scholar John Wycliffe translated it into English. Gradually the Catholic Church has increasingly encouraged laity to read, but never as much as Protestants sect laity.
8. www.swedenborg.org; www.swedenborg.com.
9. *Holy Bible*, New International Version (2011). Copyright permission regulations allow for the copying of fewer than 500 verses.
10. Bourgeault (2010).
11. http://plato.stanford.edu. An encyclopedia of philosophy.
12. *Jesus Christ Superstar*, rock opera by Andrew Lloyd Weber (1971). *Godspell*, musical by Stephen Schwartz and John-Michael Tebelak (1970). *The DaVinci code*, novel by Dan Brown (2003). *The book of love*, novel by Kathleen McGowan (2009).
13. www.lyricsondemand.com
14. www.newworldencyclopedia.org
15. Fowler (1981).
16. Perry (1970).
17. Belenky (1986).
18. Lester (2006).
19. Haskins (1993).
20. Bourgeault (2010).
21. Griffith-Jones (2008).
22. Pope Gregory I: Homily XXXIII, in 591 AD. See Ehrman (2004).

23. Newman (2005).
24. Swedenborg, *Heaven and Hell* #257; Swedenborg, *Apocalypse Explained* #586; Swedenborg, *Arcana coelestia* #720.
25. Mullan (2003). *The Magdalen sisters.* Movie about the Irish and British Catholic Church's treatment of sexually active girls.
26. Lester (2006).
27. Downing (1985).
28. Lester (2006).
29. Swedenborg (1976) *Apocalypse explained*; Swedenborg (2000) *Heaven and Hell.*
30. Belenky (1986).
31. Moody (1997).
32. Brown (2003) *The DaVinci code.*
33. Brown and Howard (2006) *The DaVinci code.* Movie.
34. Baigent (1982).
35. McGowan (2006); McGowan (2009).
36. Newman (2005).
37. Pagels (1979).
38. Pagels (1979).
39. King (2003).
40. Swedenborg (2008) *True Christianity* #508.
41. Haskins (1993).
42. Belenky (1986).
43. Camus (1942).
44. McGowan (2009).
45. McGowan (2009).
46. Israel Museum, Jerusalem, Israel.
47. Cowper (2006); Craney (2008); Hughes (2006); Markale (2001); Markale (2004); Martin (2005); Mattingly (2005).
48. Markale (2001); Markale (2004).
49. Ehrman (2004).
50. Fowler (1981).
51. Brown (2003).
52. Starbird (1993).
53. Moody (1997), p. 270.
54. Swedenborg (1984) *Arcana coelestia* #5063.
55. Swedenborg (1984) *Arcana coelestia* #9263.

56. www.heavenlydoctrines.org
57. www.monument-paris.com
58. Krathwohl (1984).
59. *Holy Bible*, New International Version (2011).
60. www.heavenlydoctrines.org; Swedenborg (1976) *Apocalypse explained* #400; Swedenborg (1984) *Arcana coelestia* #9814.
61. Moody (1997).
62. Belenky (1986).
63. Kohlberg (1976).
64. Maslow (1998).
65. Swedenborg (1976) *Apocalypse explained* # 198.
66. www.magd.ox.ac.uk
67. www.magd.ox.ac.uk
68. Fowler (1981).
69. Swedenborg (1976) *Apocalypse explained* #899.
70. Erikson (1950).
71. Fowler (1981).
72. Moody (1997).
73. Bar-Am (1998).
74. Lester (2006).
75. Moody (1997).
76. Swedenborg (1984) *Arcana coelestia* #6472.
77. Swedenborg (1995) *Charity* #1.
78. *Holy Bible*, International Version (2011).
79. *Holy Bible*, International Version (2011).
80. King (2003).
81. King (2003).
82. Ehrman (2004).
83. *Holy Bible*, International Version (2011).
84. Swedenborg (1976). *Apocalypse explained* #746.
85. Belenky (1986).
86. Belenky (1986).
87. Goldberger (1996).
88. Erikson (1950).
89. Swedenborg (1980). *Conjugial love* #100.
90. Moody (1997).
91. Swedenborg (2008). *True Christianity* #443:2.

92. Werner (2010).
93. Bonechi (2011).
94. Bonechi (2011).
95. Via Dolorosa, station VI, Veronica wipes off the face of Jesus.
96. Via Dolorosa, station VIII, Jesus speaks to the women of Jerusalem.
97. Bonechi (2011).
98. Bonechi, (2011).
99. Cohen (unknown date).
100. King (2011).

LIST OF REFERENCES AND SUGGESTED READING IN CATELGORIES:

Scholarly Reference Books about Mary Magdalene

Griffith-Jones, R. (2008) *Beloved disciple: The misunderstood legacy of Mary Magdalene, the woman closest to Jesus.* NY: Harper One.

Haskins, S. (1993). *Mary Magdalen: Myth and metaphor.* NY: Riverhead.

King, K. L. (2003). *The gospel of Mary of Magdala: Jesus and the first woman apostle.* Santa Rosa CA: Polebridge.

Starbird, M. (1993) *The woman with the alabaster jar: Mary Magdalen and the holy grail.* Rochester, VT: Bear & Co.

Popular, General References about Mary Magdalene

Carroll, J. (June 2006). Who was Mary Magdalene? *Smithsonian.* 37 (3) 108-119.

Ehrman, B. D. (2004). *Truth and fiction in the DaVinci code.* NY: Oxford University Press.

Lester, M. (2006) *The everything Mary Magdalene book: The life and legacy of Jesus' most misunderstood disciple.* Avon, MA: Adams Media.

Newman, S. (2005). *The real history behind the DaVinci Code.* NY: Berkeley Books.

Vamosh, M. F. (2007). *Women at the time of the Bible.* Israel: Palphot.

www.lyricsondemand.com Retrieved on March 1, 2011.

Historical Fiction/Novels
Some are Relevant to Mary Magdalene

Baigent, M. (1982). *Holy blood, holy grail*. NY: Random House.

Brown, D. (2003). *The DaVinci code*. NY: Doubleday.

Camus, A. (1942). *The outsider*. France: Libraire Gallimard.

Diamant, A. (1997). *The red tent*. NY: St. Martin's Press.

George, M. (2002). *Mary, called Magdalene*. NY: Penguin Books.

McGowan, K. (2006). *The expected one*. NY: Touchstone.

McGowan, K. (2009). *The book of love: Book two of the Magdalene line*. NY: Touchstone.

Slaughter, F. G. (1953). *The Galileans*. Garden City, NY: Doubleday.

Books about Gnosticism
Some are Relevant to Mary Magdalene

Ehrman, B. D. (2003). *Lost scriptures*. Oxford: University Press.

Hoeller, S. (2002). *Gnosticism*. Wheaton, IL: Quest Books.

Leloup, J. (2002). *The gospel of Mary Magdalene*. Rochester, VT: Inner Traditions

Malachi, T. (2006) *St. Mary Magdalene: The gnostic tradition of the holy bride*. Woodbury, MN: Llewellyn.

Matkin, J. M. (2005). *The gnostic gospels*. NY: Alpha.

Meyer, M. (translator) (1984) *The secret teachings of Jesus.* NY: Random.

Nahmad, C. & Bailey, M. (2006) *The secret teachings of Mary Magdalene.* London: Watkins.

Pagels, E. (1979). *The gnostic gospels.* NY: Random.

Robinson, J. (Ed.) (1990). *The Nag Hammadi library.* San Francisco: Harper.

Goddess Worship, Divine Feminine, New-Age Spirituality Relevant to Mary Magdalene

Bourgeault, C. (2010) *The meaning of Mary Magdalene: Discovering the woman at the heart of Christianity.* NY: Random House.

Houston, S. (2006). *Invoking Mary Magdalene: Accessing the wisdom of the divine feminine.* Boulder, CO: Sounds True

Norton, J. (2005). *The Mary Magdalene within.* NY: iUniverse.

Woolger, J. B. & Woolger, R. J. (1987). *The goddess within.* NY: Ballantine.

http://www.spiritbride.org/A/spiritbride/index2.html Retrieved on March 1, 2011.

Southern France, Cathars Relevant to Mary Magdalene

Cowper, M. (2006). *Cathar castles.* Westminster, MD: Osprey Press.
Craney, G. (2008). *The fire and the light: A novel of the Cathars and the lost teachings of Christ.* Los Angeles: Brigid.

Hughes, N. (2006) *The Cathar legacy*. Pyradice Publishing. Lulu Press (online printer).

Markale, J. (2001). *Montsegur and the mystery of the Cathars*. Rochester, VT: Inner Traditions.

Markale, J. (2004). *The Church of Mary Magdalene: The sacred feminine and the treasure of Rennes-le-Chateau*. Rochester, VT: Inner Traditions.

Martin, S. (2005) *The Cathars*. Edison, NJ: Cartwell.

Mattingly, A. (2005). *Walks in the Cathar region*. UK: Cicerone.

Theological References
Relevant to Mary Magdalene

Currie, S. (2004). "Mary Magdalene, companion of the Lord." Unpublished manuscript. (see http://www.bridgewaternewchurch.org)

David, W. (1964). *Hymnal for schools and families*. Bryn Athyn, PA: General Church of the New Jerusalem.

The Holy Bible, New International Version. (2011). Colorado Springs: Biblica, Inc.

King, K. (April 2011). Theta Alpha Banquet address. *Theta Alpha journal*. 13(5)3-9.

Swanson, V.G. (2006). *Dynasty of the holy grail: Mormonism's Sacred Bloodline*. Springville, Utah: Cedar Fort, Inc.

Swedenborg, E. (1976). *Apocalypse explained*. NY: Swedenborg Foundation.
Swedenborg, E. (1980). *Conjugial love*. NY: Swedenborg Foundation.

Swedenborg, E. (1984). *Arcana coelestia*. NY: Swedenborg Foundation.

Swedenborg, E. (1995). *Charity*. West Chester, PA: Swedenborg Foundation.

Swedenborg, E. (2000). *Heaven and Hell*. West Chester, PA: Swedenborg Foundation.

Swedenborg, E. (2008). *True Christianity*. West Chester, PA: Swedenborg Foundation.

Werner, S. S. (2010). "Sincerity and severity." *New Church life*. 130 (10) 396-402.

www.catholictradition.org/Saints/signs2.htm Retrieved on March 1, 2011.

www.heavenlydoctrines.org Retrieved on March 1, 2011. (Search here for sermons and articles in *New Church life* on the Easter story, *The Da Vinci code* and Mary Magdalene.)

www.swedenborg.com Retrieved on March 1, 2011.

www.swedenborg.org Retrieved on March 1, 2011.

Psychological References

Belenky, M., Clinchy, B., Goldberger, N. & Tarule, J. (1986). *Women's ways of knowing*. NY: Basic Books.

Bloom, B. S., Englehart, M.B., Furst, E.J., Hill, W.H. & Krathwohl, D.R. (Eds.). (1956). *Taxonomy of educational objectives. The classification of educational goals. Handbook I: Cognitive domain*. NY: McKay.
Downing, N. E. & Roush, K.L. (1985). From passive

acceptance to active commitment. *The counseling psychologist.* 13 (4) 695-709.

Erikson, E. H. (1950). *Childhood and society.* NY: W.W. Norton.

Fowler, J. W. (1981). *Stages of faith.* San Francisco: Harper.

Gilligan, C. (1982). *In a different voice.* Cambridge, MA: Harvard University Press.

Goldberger, N., Tarule, J., Clinchy, B. & Belenky, M. (Eds.) (1996). *Knowledge, difference, and power: Essays inspired by women's ways of knowing.* NY: Basic Books.

Kohlberg, L. (1976). Moral stages and moralizing: The cognitive-developmental approach. In T. Lickona (Ed.) *Moral development and behavior.* NY: Holt, Rinehart & Winston.

Krathwohl, D.R., Bloom, B.S. & Masia, B.B. (1964). *Taxonomy of educational objectives. Handbook II: Affective domain.* NY: McKay.

Maslow, A. (1998). *Towards a psychology of being.* NJ: Wiley.

Paloutzian, R. F. (Editor) (2005). *Handbook of the psychology of religion and spirituality.* NY: Guilford.

Perry, W.G. (1970). *Forms of intellectual and ethical development in the college years: A scheme.* NY: Holt, Rinehart & Winston.

Philosophical References

http://plato.stanford.edu Retrieved March 1, 2011.

Moody, H. R. (1997). *The five stages of the soul.* NY: Anchor Books.

www.encyclopedia.org Retrieved on March 1, 2011.

Travel Books and Websites

Bar-Am, A. (1998). *Beyond the walls: Churches of Jerusalem.* Jerusalem, Israel: Ahva Press.

Bonechi, C. (2011). *Jerusalem.* Italy: Bonechi Books.

Cohen, D. (Date unknown). *In the footsteps of Jesus.* Israel: Doko Media.

Georgiou, A. (Ed.) (2010). *Israel.* London: Insight Guides.

Glenn, E.B. (1971). *The Bryn Athyn cathedral: Building of a church.* NY: C. Harrison Conroy Publishers and General Church of the New Jerusalem.

Inman, N. (Ed.) (2010). *Jerusalem, Israel, Petra & Sinai.* London: DK Eyewitness Travel.

www.magd.ox.ac.uk Retrieved on March 1, 2011.

www.monument-paris.com Retrieved on March 1, 2011.

Motion Pictures and Television
Relevant to Mary Magdalene

Howard, R. (Director). (2006). *The DaVinci code.* (Motion picture). Japan and United States: Sony Pictures.

Marvizon, M. (Writer & Producer). (2004). *Mary Magdalene: The hidden apostle.* (Television series episode). In M. Marvizon (Producer), Biography. United States: A&E Television Networks.

Mullan, P. (Director). (2003). *The Magdalen sisters*. (Motion picture). England: Momentum Pictures Ltd.

(Search for additional films on www.netflix.com)

Mullan, P. (Director). (2003). *The Magdalen sisters*. (Motion picture). England: Momentum Pictures Ltd.

(Search for additional films on www.netflix.com)